LISTEN HERE!

D1617387

Listen Here!

The Art and Spirituality of Listening

MEGAN McKENNA

Paulist Press
New York / Mahwah, NJ

Cover image by moodboard/Thinkstockphotos.com
Cover design by Phyllis Campos
Book design by Lynn Else

Library of Congress Cataloging-in-Publication Data

McKenna, Megan.
    Listen here! : the art and spirituality of listening / Megan McKenna.
      pages cm
    Includes bibliographical references.
    ISBN 978-0-8091-4921-6 (pbk. : alk. paper) — ISBN 978-1-58768-485-2 (ebook)
    1. Listening—Religious aspects—Christianity. I. Title.
    BV4647.L56M35 2016
    248.4`6—dc23

                                      2015023130

ISBN 978-0-8091-4921-6 (paperback)
ISBN 978-1-58768-485-2 (e-book)

Published by Paulist Press in 2016
997 Macarthur Boulevard
Mahwah, New Jersey 07430

www.paulistpress.com

Printed and bound in the
United States of America

With gratitude beyond words
and great delight working with you
and dwelling with you awhile...and listening!
Jenny and Jim; Paul and Mary-Elizabeth and Dave
Michael and Dianne
Lynette
Julianne
Tony and Jan
David
and
✢ John Dew
✢ Patrick Dunn
✢ Denis Browne
✢ Colin Campbell
✢ Charles Drennan
✢ Peter Cullinane
✢ Barry Jones
The Aotearoa New Zealand Bishops
AROHANUI

CONTENTS

INTRODUCTION

"Everything's got to do with listening."
—W. S. Merwin

*"Incline your ear to me; make haste
to rescue me!"*
—Psalm 31:2

This book started, oddly enough, with one line that I sometimes use to introduce workshops on storytelling and the Scriptures. The workshop title is "God Is Listening. What Are We Saying?" People are often startled to realize that I'm not talking primarily about praying to God; I'm talking about a long, enduring, deepening relationship between us and God—in the plural— meaning that we are listened to, as a people, as one voice. Individual voices are all there, but what do we sound like as one voice crying out (since in our humanness, we are all one), wanting not only God to hear and listen to us—to attend to us—but everyone else to hear and listen to us as well.

I then was asked to do a series of all-day workshops for hospital chaplains in a group of ten hospitals in an urban area. The chaplains who attended came from a range of religious traditions: Judaism, Christianity, Islam, Buddhism, Hinduism, Native American religions,

1

and those who described themselves as eclectic, non-aligned or nontraditional, even spiritual, just not religious. The workshops were done twice so that everyone could attend, half the group covering the other half's duties for two days, and then switching.

These were people who spent a good portion of their days hearing and overhearing conversations between people in difficult, extraordinary situations, and also hearing silences that ranged from awkward and tense, to deep communion, to just empty. Many admitted that they had difficulty hearing and listening to some people: those of other faiths; those who were belligerent, angry, adding to the stress of illness, violence, accidents, and life-threatening situations; those that were in the last moments they were sharing with loved ones or strangers. The physical ability to hear was hard also—often necessitating intimacy and physical closeness to someone they had no prior contact with, many knowing these were the last breaths of a person. And listening—somehow taking the words, the sighs and senses of terror, pain, loneliness, and isolation, visceral needs to be heard, to confess and ask forgiveness, to be assured and told they were loved—was even more difficult. All agreed the hardest and most humbling part of their connections with people was the silence—of attending with utmost care to someone, saying nothing and yet listening to that person as though they were the only person in the world. So we dealt with seven levels of listening—basically the opening chapters of this book—and then from those experiences, discussion of other ways of listening expanded out and stretched into other places and people.

Finding a title for the book proved elusive! There are sayings and one-liners galore about hearing and listening, but how could I capture layers of meaning in three or four words that would immediately engage and draw people into the contents of the book? In writing a book, I usually begin with the title or a phrase that has layers of meaning that I can call mine and play with, but with this book, there was a surfeit—too many suggestions. Finally, after the book was nearly finished, after trying to glean ideas from friends around the world, I settled on the title: *Listen Here!*, playing on the sound of the words and associations with *hear, here,* and *listen* (the word *silent* hidden in *listen*) and making it a command, a plea, and an exhortation with the punctuation mark *!*.

I am writing this book while I'm sixty-eight to sixty-nine years of age, and I am acutely aware of the state of my own hearing—continually trying to hear and comprehend other languages, or those who speak English as a second or third language, in large crowds, with any number of voices: tentative, soft, strident, reflective, hesitant, emotional, and at varying distances from me, along with a range of physical settings—school gyms, classrooms, arenas, outdoors, in rooms with dirt floors, and places of worship—all of which strongly affects acoustics. Added to this hearing and listening is technology—double mikes for taping, relaying to other rooms, to remote TVs, and to augment sound. Often during sessions I wonder if the issue is their level of speaking or my inability to hear. I also have my hearing checked periodically—especially after I return from a foreign country and have experienced more difficulty in hearing and repeating for others what someone says in the group. As with most people around the age of seventy, my own hearing is becoming thin, but not yet at the point of needing technical assistance; that will soon become a reality.

This sense of hearing and the connection it engenders that is essential is only the beginning. The rest of the book is listening beyond the words. A man by the name of Peter F. Drucker (that's all I know of him, since the line was on a sign in a film lab) once said, "The most important thing in communication is to hear what isn't being said." This is the subject of many of the chapters, taken from various angles.

There is a story a friend shared with me—he has used it himself to speak about the concept of what listening is with others. It happened to him more than twenty-five years ago, but its impact has been lasting.

Once upon a time, there was a monastery. Their financial support came primarily from an egg business. It was a time-consuming and exhausting job: raising the chickens, gathering the eggs, processing them, and selling them to local restaurants and supermarkets. Some of the job, like collecting the eggs, was done every day, but processing them and getting them ready to transport was done just two days a week. The monastery had ten thousand chickens which lay about eight or nine thousand eggs a day! They would have to collect them, wash them, weigh and grade them, arrange them in cardboard flats, stack the flats into cartons, and then load them onto trucks to take into town. The young monk's job (we'll call him Joe) was to do the processing and make sure the eggs were ready to be delivered by the man who helped them out, Tom. One day Tom brought along his son, Joshua, who was about four years old. They had been working and one batch had been processed with no trouble. Tom was working in another area of the barn, and Joe returned to start the next set. Entering the barn where the flats were stacked, he was dismayed to find that the flats, two hundred of them to a stack, were strewn all over the floor, making any work impossible. Joshua had started playing around and had been tossing them, Frisbee-style, in every direction out into the middle of the floor.

Joe approached Josh and asked him nicely to start stacking the flats up again so that he could use them. To his utter shock, Josh's answer was a flat no. Now, monks are not used to being told no, or if that is the answer, it usually comes with an excuse or a sense that it will be done later. So Joe knelt on the floor and tried to be rational, explaining why he needed the flats off the floor. Would Josh do this for him and help him? Again, the answer was just no. Then he tried to use his authority and told him, "This is how we do it here." Again the answer was just a plain and simple and unequivocal no. Next, Joe tried the ruse of "As soon as we can finish this, you and your dad can go into town. So would you please restack the flats?" The answer didn't change: "No."

With that, Joe went to talk with Tom to see if he could get Joshua to start stacking. He explained the situation to Tom, and Tom came and had a look, "Oh, I see

your problem." Joe, frustrated, said, "All he keeps saying, no matter what I say and how I ask him to stack
them, is no." It was Tom's explanation that changed
everything. "Joe, you have to know that when he says
no like that, what he means is 'I don't know how to do
it,' and he's too proud to tell you that he doesn't know,
so he just says, "No." With that, Joe went back to Joshua
and sat on the floor and started restacking the flats. In
no time at all, Joshua was beside him, stacking the flats.
After a short while, Joe got up and said, "I need to go
check on the chickens. Do you think you can stack
these by yourself?" The answer was quick: "Sure!" This
experience has stayed with Joe and led to his knowing
that listening isn't about hearing only, but about listening with intuition, knowledge, heart, soul, and everything in us.

Other chapters in this book look outside our own
hearing, our listening beyond our own bodies, to others
and the world beyond us—out into the universe. They
are about the art of learning beyond our own experience
through others and the world. As Maya Angelou wrote,
"Words mean more than what is set down on paper. It
takes the human voice to infuse them with the shades of
deeper meaning."[1] Another woman shares this sense of
listening beyond our usual parameters—Terry Tempest
Williams. Williams writes of her time in Rwanda and
what she has heard; those she listened to and what
opened her to other ways of listening. She is a writer par
excellence, but in order to be a writer, you must spend
a good deal of time just listening to others.

There is a common phrase in Rwanda, "He has a good heart." How does one know? We know the quality of another's heart through her voice. Not the sound, although it is a cue. Not through words, although they present an idea. I most often feel the tenor of another's heart through tone and the feeling that enters my body when they speak.

"Once you know that you have a voice," Louis said, "it's no longer the voice that matters, but what is behind the voice."

Louis has improved the quality of my listening.

In Rwanda, they say a person's silence can be heard as a lion's roar.[2]

This piece is from Williams's *When Women Were Birds*, a book that has accompanied me for a number of months, questioning me and dropping bits of wisdom and wonder into my life while helping me to ask questions and listen from many new angles. Its contents and author are truly gifts for mind, heart, and soul.

There are chapters on silence, music and noise, our bodies and the body of earth among the bodies of the universe–drawing us out into layers of sound and the arts of listening beyond words and their contents. These chapters hope to extend our range and deepen our abilities of perception. A saying from Argentina is "The voice of the people is the voice of God," indicating that to whom we listen is as crucial as the listening itself. What we listen to impacts us as well. "Did you know that trees talk? Well they do. They talk to each other, and they'll talk to you if you listen. I have learned a lot from trees; sometimes about the weather, sometimes about animals, sometimes about the Great Spirit."[3]

There is a chapter on the dark, on night as holy—a place we need to enter and approach with awe and ears and hearts attuned. The poet Wendell Berry writes of the dark as one who knows it and wants to share its depth and riches. Instead of being a negative, the absence of light, it is for him of equal worth. It "blooms and sings" in its own way, and one can understand the light only by understanding the dark.

> To go in the dark with a light is to know the
>   light.[4]

At the end of each chapter, there are suggestions for further mulling, wondering, questing, and reflection, and sometimes a practice to begin that I hope takes you, the reader, further into your own hearing, listening, and becoming attentive. As I tried to end each chapter, I was acutely aware that each could be the basis of a book in itself! So, these thoughts are presented as jumping-off places and open doors to begin a journey or a process of developing, learning, and practicing another aspect of the art of listening.

A number of people have asked me, in the course of writing this book and presenting portions of it in work-shops and sermons, talks, and so on, if it's a religious book, or if it's for religious people. I started answering with a line from the jazz musician, John Coltrane: "My goal is to live the truly religious life and express it in my music."[5] The word *religious* comes from a root word *religio*—meaning to bind or to tie together. It can be likened to a medical term that describes the binding together of muscles, sinews, tissue, veins, and bones, especially around the major joints: knees, elbows, hips, spine, and neck, that allow for movement and keep us bending and mobile. There are the seven major religions of the world, and then there are the limitless ways of being religious and practicing one's belief in concert with others. I dwell in the tradition of being Catholic, Christian, and a believer in the God who has so many names, and yet is Nameless, knowable in all things, and ultimately the Unknown. I abide in the mysteries of the Trinity, the incarnation, the resurrection, and the Spirit that binds all humans and all things together in the universe as one and holy—one song, one poem, one psalm, one silent, listening Presence. This book is for everyone, anyone who seeks to hear, to listen, and to become more human in the image of the One who is listening to us all. It asks, "What are we saying?" Then it probes deeper still: "Are we listening back?" *Listen here!*

1

LISTENING – HEARING

As all the Heavens were a Bell
And Being but an Ear...

—Emily Dickinson

Hear Ye! Hear Ye!
NOW HEAR THIS!
Take Heed.
The Doors! The Doors! BE ATTENTIVE!

—Orthodox Liturgy

Can you hear me?
Do you hear what I hear?

—Traditional Christmas Carol

Hear, O LORD, and answer me,
for I am poor and needy.

—Psalm 86:1

Give ear to my words, O Lord,
consider my sighing.
Listen to my cry for help,
my King and my God,
for to you I pray.
In the morning, O Lord, you hear my voice;
in the morning I lay my requests before you
*   and wait in expectation.*

—Psalm 5:1–3

Hear, O Lord, my righteous plea: listen to
*   my cry,*
Give ear to my prayer.

—Psalm 17:1

To you I call, O Lord my Rock:
do not turn a deaf ear to me.

—Psalm 28:1

We have heard with our ears, O God,
our fathers have told us
what you did in their days,
in days long ago.

—Psalm 44:1

Hear this, all you peoples:
listen all who live in this world,

both low and high,
rich and poor alike:
My mouth will speak words of wisdom;
the utterance from my heart will give
* understanding.*
I will turn my ear to a proverb;
with the harp I will expound my riddle.
*   —Psalm 49:1–4*

Hear my cry, O God;
listen to my prayer.
From the ends of the earth I call to you,
I call as my heart grows faint.
*   —Psalm 61:1–2a*

I love the LORD, for he heard my voice;
he heard my cry for mercy.
Because he turned his ear to me,
I will call on him as long as I live.
*   —Psalm 116:1–2*

Out of the depths I cry to you, O LORD.
Lord, hear my voice!
Let your ears be attentive
to my cry for mercy!
*   —Psalm 130:1–2*

HEARING

The act of hearing—sound, all sorts of sounds, enter our ears involuntarily. In today's reality, practically anywhere in the world, there is a multiplicity of sounds. What is external in the world is one side of hearing. The other side is the capacity of the individual to actually register sound, to hear. It is surprising how many people are hearing impaired and how many impediments to hearing there are all around us. Scientists, psychologists, audiologists, musicians, anyone who works with the elderly or speaks in public in large groups are unanimous in trying to tell the population at large that many of us are suffering from audibility problems, but many are reluctant to acknowledge any difficulty in hearing.

Hearing is a physical activity. Inside our ears, we collect signals that are sent to parts of our brains, and there are resultant sounds that register. Since we have two ears, it is happening simultaneously as we absorb sound, though not necessarily to the same degree of accuracy or volume. Each of our ears has a hearing range that changes over time and inevitably begins to deteriorate and lessen in capacity. This gift of hearing is separate from and yet connected to being able to perceive vibrations in music, pounding noise, echoes, and certain levels of voices.

A couple of years ago, I was in South Africa at a conference on religion and education and part of the entertainment one evening was a performance by a group of young native dancers, all hearing impaired. I happened to be sitting within a few feet of the stage, near the sound system that was playing the music, and close to the dancers and their teacher who was acting as their director. She sat on the end of the first row in the audience. It was fascinating, amazing, and deeply moving to watch them in sync, watching the director's movements and sensing the vibrations from the music and their own feet on the stage floor in rhythm as one. They moved so gracefully, powerfully, quickly, sure of themselves, intent on appearing as one body in harmony. We were hearing sound and they were feeling vibrations, and both the audience and the dancers were hearing with our whole bodies, all our senses coming together to deepen the experience. There was awed silence when they finished and then thunderous applause—and they stomped their feet in response to our clapping and verbal praise. Later when I was speaking with the director, a woman in her thirties with some hearing impairment, we tried to talk about the difference between hearing the music and sensing the vibrations—being able to hear and being deaf. Someone overheard us and told us that in many languages—Italian and African dialects, for example—there is no difference in the words used to describe what we were trying to fathom. The word in Italian that means "to hear" is *sentire* and when the same verb is used in the reflexive form, *sentirsi*, it means "to sense" or "to feel." Many of the dancers were adamant that they were not deaf! They just didn't hear the same way we do. They hear through their senses since they have problems hearing with just their one sense—hearing.

This issue of hearing loss is becoming more universal. In the United States, the statistics state that more than forty-eight million people suffer from some level of hearing loss. In Great Britain, the number is ten million. Very few lose all hearing; most lose one or more frequencies and other frequencies are lessened. The reasons are varied: aging, the constant din of outside, background noises, the tendency to turn the volume of technology up to deafening levels in public places, as well as the spread of personal listening through digital/electronic devices with ear buds. This kind of noise or sound that we absorb unthinkingly has resulted in what has been labeled the "dumbing down of our hearing" by Rupert Taylor, a noise consultant from Suffolk, England, in his book *Noise*. In addition to sound itself causing hearing loss, there are infections and diseases as causes; often young children lose hearing during an infection and sometimes their hearing returns weakened, due to fluid buildup in the middle ear. New studies reveal that obesity, especially in the years from ages twelve to twenty, is causing hearing loss across all ranges and frequencies and that young people are twice as likely to have one-sided low frequency hearing loss.

Smoking and being exposed to second-hand smoke nearly double the risk of hearing loss, especially if your mother smoked during pregnancy. Taking certain drugs like ibuprofen or acetaminophen more than twice a week is found to increase hearing loss. The American Speech-Language-Hearing Association has concluded that certain types of antibiotics, chemotherapy, aspirin (in large doses), antimalarial drugs, and certain diuretics used in kidney and heart disease can damage hearing.

Much of this hearing loss is preventable. In *AARP*

The Magazine, it was reported that 85 percent of Americans over fifty said that their hearing is important to them, but only 43 percent had gotten their hearing checked out during the past five years.[1] They asked questions and compiled the following data. Thirty-two percent said they thought their hearing was excellent. Twenty percent said they have difficulty hearing and they've gotten treatment for it. Fifteen percent said they know they have difficulty hearing, but they haven't done anything about it, and 32 percent said their hearing isn't as good as it used to be or could be but they don't need any treatment. Another study commented that generally speaking, women are losing their low range of hearing, and men, conversely, are losing their higher ranges of hearing—resulting in the difficulty of men and women hearing one another.

There is another kind of deafness called *psychogenic* that was noticed after World War I and has continued to increase in numbers and intensity throughout the wars of recent decades. Exposed to bombs exploding, guns firing, missiles, aircraft flying low, detonation of IEDs, and the constant screaming of human voices has resulted in hearing loss and more, with soldiers becoming mute as well. This condition of being mute and unable to speak can often be reversed but not in all cases. The U.S. Army now calculates that nearly two-thirds of frontline troops in Iraq and Afghanistan have suffered hearing damage. More disturbing is what has followed from this reality.

That in turn has led to the science of psycho-acoustics or, in its more sinister form, "white

torture," overloading suspects' senses by playing drills or death-metal music at extreme volume for hours on end. They say shamans can
sing a man to death; now the government is
having a go at it, too.[2]

Many people are reluctant to admit hearing loss.
Because of noise levels and constant background
sounds, we have instinctively learned to block out what
we don't want to hear, or if it is disturbing our sleep, we
resort to ear plugs. We can censor out what registers. We
are aware of how much we block, only when we look for
a certain sound and have difficulty locking in on it in
the midst of all the other competing ones, for instance,
when we seek out the voice of someone we know in a
crowd, or our child crying, and so on.

Hearing is an amazing feat! It involves the ear, the
nervous system, the brain, and connections among the
three. Then it involves ranges of frequencies: high, mid,
and low levels of sound waves. Then there are two kinds
of hearing: conductive (vibrations made by sound traveling through the body—listening to the music at a concert or sometimes a specific musical instrument, or a
power drill on the sidewalk) and sensorineural (when
sound passes through and is processed by the inner ear
and cochlea).

There are many ways to conceal the fact that you
are missing sounds and having difficulty in hearing.
There are many excuses to blame it on, outside factors
rather than internal realities. I do a great deal of public
speaking, often with microphones that amplify my voice

to others, while at the same time recording my words for CDs, DVDs, and so on. My style is to talk back and forth with the audience, and when someone in the audience speaks, I try to repeat what they say for the recording as well as everyone else in the room. I first noticed difficulty in catching all of what people were saying during an engagement in Japan and began to panic—I have to be able to hear what people are saying! When I mentioned it to some of the people I was with, they laughed and said, "It's not you. It's us. We are trained to not draw attention to ourselves in many instances. Try asking the people to speak up." That did work in many cases. A few years later, more recently, I was having trouble in New Zealand and again thought, "I'm losing my ability to hear." Again I was told, "No, we speak very softly. We don't like to stand out in crowds."

In reflecting on the experiences of having difficulty catching all the words that people are saying, I noticed that I have become incredibly good at filling in what people are saying by using my other senses. As a speaker who tells stories, preaches, and theologizes, I often tell my listeners that "your eyes are connected to your ears." I listen intently to intonation, inflection, pitch, which words are louder than others, pace, rhythm, and cadences (almost as though they are singing), and have come to realize that many people drop their voices and end sentences by saying the last words very soft, almost inaudibly. So I cock my head, turn one or the other ear to them, shift my body, lean forward, and sometimes in desperation walk down the aisle to get closer to them, as well as read their lips and facial expressions and body language, what they do with their hands and arms, the way they stand—anything that will allow me to hear/see them better. I repeat what they say, trying for word-for-word repetition to make sure we are all hearing the same words.

Many of my friends are musicians and they are quick to tell me that it is in listening to music—raw music, without amplification—that can reveal immediately whether or not you are losing specific ranges of frequencies and hearing. You can pick up after listening to the music that something is missing—though it is hard to put your finger on exactly what is gone. The more instruments and/or voices that are involved in a piece, the more gaps and holes will be apparent.

Another outside factor that contributes to being heard and hearing is the way many groups (small ones, but good-sized ones as well) structure their environments—primarily in circles. The larger the circle, the more difficult it becomes to hear. If anyone has any hearing loss, it is noticeable when they cannot hear at a distance or across a circle. It can be equally as difficult to hear the people sitting on either side of us, since we can't see their faces, lips, and so on, unless we turn to face them. Whenever we speak, but especially in circles, we project our voices out and away from our bodies. In small, intimate gatherings, people have a tendency to lower their voices, making hearing even more difficult.

Another problem with hearing loss is that many people don't want to hear certain things or certain people! It's just easier to tune out anything that is distasteful, annoying, angers you, or anyone you disagree with. Sometimes we just want to ignore reality and go inside ourselves so that we do not have to deal with whatever and whoever is there demanding attention. Sometimes, with some people, it's just easier to be selectively deaf and not make any effort to hear them or relate to them. It's easier to tune them out.

These are thoughts on hearing—just the process of being able to absorb sound and take in what is out there—noise, music, sound, and voices. There is a quantum leap between the ability to hear and what we call *listening*. What we hear is powerful, but the ability to listen is even more powerful. We want to be heard—and yet, even more, we want someone to listen to us. The act of listening is an art form, a discipline, and a gift beyond reckoning. But just because we can physically hear doesn't mean we know how to hear someone out, to listen to them, or to listen to anything or nothing at all.

Perhaps to begin to bridge the gap between what it means to hear and what it means to listen, a story might be in order. It is an experience that I had more than thirty years ago when I first moved to Albuquerque, New Mexico. At the time, I was working with many Native American tribes, and after teaching and sharing stories with them, they began to share their traditional stories with me. A medicine man, probably in his mid-seventies, told me he'd take me on and teach me some basics about storytelling, about hearing and listening, singing, and the rituals of his community so that we could work better together and I could better understand the people. Every couple of weeks, he would come in from the pueblo and we'd meet on Central Avenue in downtown Albuquerque. The street was a main cross-city thoroughfare for interstate traffic that comes off the main routes to stop and eat or stay overnight in motels. It was a street of shops, fast food restaurants, diners, movie theaters, tattoo parlors, and every sort of coffee place for folks to meet. Essentially, it was loud and noisy with the passing of cars—low riders bouncing and sputtering along the road, semis, radios/music blaring, and people talking. This was where we'd walk and he'd talk and sometimes ask me questions and I'd answer—watching and listening to everything around us at the same time. It was always a bit exhausting, especially in summer when it was hot, dry, windy, and there was the added pollution of the street to contend with.

We had been talking and the conversation had halted for a few minutes when he suddenly stopped dead in his tracks and lifted his head and looked away from me and the street. He said, "Do you hear that?" I stopped and became conscious of trying to hear—something—but I had no idea what it was I was trying to discern among all the layers of sound in the street. I tried and then said, "What am I listening for?" He looked at me oddly and patiently said, "That...that...can't you hear it?" I tried again—and I heard a lot of things—peoples' conversations that I'd just ignored and put in the back of my mind; the song on the radio as a car passed by with its windows wide open, the voices of children laughing and fighting too. Again I asked, "What is it I'm listening for?"

This time he grabbed me by the arm and dragged me running across the street, in between cars and trucks, and we moved another twenty yards down on the opposite sidewalk. We stopped in front of a concrete planter. Originally, there had been a bush and some flowers in it, but in the heat of August, there were only scraggly weeds, very dead, and dry dirt. "There!" he said. "That!" I looked and listened and there was nothing. *Listen Here!* Then, finally, when I saw it, I could hear it—crickets! They were chirping away and scratching their legs together. I was stunned—he had heard that from across the street? No way! He was laughing at me by now, and I was looking at him askance too. I said to him, "Is this some Indian thing? How could you hear that from over there, with all the noise of the traffic and people? How?" Again, I got that look he'd give me when I was slow or thick or both, and he said, "It all depends what you're listening for!" I took that in and tried to digest it. I'd heard the words he said, but I wasn't all that sure I believed him.

Then he said, "Look, I'll show you." He had the habit of filling the pockets of his overalls with quarters. He'd buy ice cream cones for any of the young ones he met on the street that he knew—or knew him—from the reservation. He took two handfuls of quarters from his deep pockets and just threw them across the sidewalk. I couldn't believe it—everyone stopped going in both directions. Conversations ended abruptly, people shouted, "Hey, man, you for real?" Within moments every one of those coins had been grabbed up. He looked at me again and said, "See, it all depends what you're listening for!" In that moment I began to learn the difference between hearing and listening, between listening to and listening for, and listening with meaning and understanding.

All around us, the world is filled with sound, words, music, cacophony, dissonance, rhythms, conversations, cries, laughter. What are we listening for? Listening is hearing with the inner ear. Listening is hearing with the heart. Listening is hearing with one's soul. Listening needs another, some relationship, some engagement or interaction. Listening and being listened to takes hearing and moves it into a realm of energy and power that sounds out what it means to be human and to relate. Listening reveals and opens more than just our ears to what is outside, beyond us, within us, and in others and the earth. Listening is learned. It is an art form, a discipline, a way of communication and relating. Now, we can begin—to listen.

Years ago, I heard this story based on an experience that actually happened:

Once upon a time, a large Lutheran congregation gathered together to talk about hiring a new minister. The present one was retiring, and while they were sad to be losing him, they were excited about finding someone to replace him, about trying something new. The candidates were honed down to just three, one of them being a woman. It was the first time they even thought of having a woman minister. In the end, she was the one chosen because she was a superb preacher.

The first Sunday morning came when she would preach, and the church was packed, standing room only. She was superb! Everyone was elated. After the service, over coffee and doughnuts, all the talk was about the sermon. It was based on the Scripture text for the day, laced with various commentaries, a story or two that engaged everyone, allusions to poetry, a piece of music that coordinated with the songs in the rest of the service, and pastoral applications to all the groups in the church. They couldn't stop praising it and the new minister, and everyone parted saying they couldn't wait to hear next Sunday's sermon.

The next Sunday arrived and the place was again packed, with a lot of new people: members of family that didn't always go, strangers who had heard about the sermon, and those curious to see what all the talk was about. Once again, the sermon was great—but it was a good couple of minutes into the sermon before anyone began to realize—that it was the exact sermon as the week before. People noticed it at different points—when the piece that had registered most with them was repeated again, almost word for word. Others didn't realize it until near the end and the connections to the songs didn't change. A few never noticed at all until it was pointed out to them, and the newcomers thought it was grand. Again after the service, the talk was all about the sermon—they realized how much they'd missed the first time through it and some swore there were new pieces inserted in the original text. The next week, they were back to the usual folks on Sunday morning and they were both amazed and some a bit annoyed that the sermon was the same one, yet again. This was the third time! Some made excuses for her—it was her first weeks in a huge urban parish and she had meetings, and to get acquainted with people, and all the groups that met in the church, new programs, and so on. Others were a bit more blunt—when was she going to come up with something new?

All week long, many wondered what next Sunday's sermon would be like, and the fourth Sunday, many didn't know what to do when it was the same thing again!

This continued for six weeks. Finally, many of the church members met with the vestry—the church elders and officials—and said that something had to be done immediately. This couldn't go on. At the next meeting, they had to bring it up and ask her point-blank when she was going to have a new sermon. They were more than tired of hearing the old one, and they couldn't live on it—not one more time. Enough was enough. The meeting was awkward, reports were given and she gave hers as well on what she'd been doing; the people she was meeting and her initial reactions to being the new pastor with them. Finally, someone stood up and blurted out, "The people want to know when you're going to present a new sermon. They're tired of hearing the same one over and over again. They know you've been busy getting settled in and that it takes a long time to prepare a sermon, but they can't hear what you're saying anymore. Everyone is agreed, they've bled every thought out of the one you've been giving over and over again."

The young woman pastor didn't seem bothered at all by the question and people's uneasiness. She looked around the room with a slight smile on her face and said, "I'll give another sermon when I know they have heard this one. I will know that they have listened and taken it to heart when they begin to practice and live out in their lives together what they have heard on Sunday.

So, you can tell them that there will be a fresh new sermon when they hear and get this one!"

It's a grand story! What is said and heard is one thing. What is not said is another. What has been taken to heart–heard with the heart–is another thing altogether, for each person hearing and for the whole people listening.

Chuang-Tzu, an ancient Chinese philosopher and teacher, described this process of hearing and listening long ago:

> The hearing that is only in the ears is one thing. The hearing of understanding is another. But the hearing of the spirit is not limited to any one faculty, to the ear or the mind. Hence it demands emptiness of all of the faculties. And when the faculties are empty, the whole being listens. There is then a direct grasp of what is right there before you that can never be heard with the ear or understood with the mind.

This is the hearing, the listening, and the openness that is where we begin this book, and the art of listening, the exercise of learning, and relearning how to hear and how to listen. *Listen Here!*

REFLECTIONS AND PRACTICES

1. How well do you hear? Have you gotten your ability to hear tested lately? If not, make an appointment to do so immediately.

2. "Hearing is how we touch at a distance," stated Susan Stewart.[3] How often do you rely on "touching at a distance," and what are some of the drawbacks of this kind of hearing, as well as its positive effects? Is there someone you relate to—at a distance, primarily through hearing? How do you think this has affected your relationship?

3. Make a list of people, and then things, that you love to hear and then another list of people you dread hearing and sounds that repulse or annoy you. Be sure to include kinds of music in your lists. Then, alongside your choices, try to express what it is that lies within the sounds that cause you to react in such a way.

2

BEGINNING

To hear something asks very little of us.
To listen places our entire being on notice.
—Terry Tempest Williams

Listening is a skill and an art form, a discipline that can be learned, rediscovered, and enhanced. A study on listening done by the University of Missouri Extension and published by Dick Lee and Delmar Hatesohl is fascinating in its findings. Although the data was shared in 1993, it is worth looking at as a reference point. They studied listening in relation to other communication skills. Other studies confirmed that we spend about 70 to 80 percent of our waking hours in some form of communication.[1] This communication breaks down as 9 percent writing, 16 percent reading, 30 percent speaking, and about 45 percent listening. The end result of the study was that "most of us are poor and inefficient listeners."[2] Now, in 2014, more than two decades later, with the onslaught of new individual and public technologies, how much more of our time is spent in listening?

One reality that contributes to poor listening is that we can think faster than anyone can speak. We speak about 125 words a minute but we have the capacity to think at about 400 words a minute, though researchers are reluctant to say that we actually think that fast on a regular basis. However, when we're in a usual conversation, we're only using about 25 percent of our brain capacity on listening—and so we have all that other capacity to be doing other things with, while we're listening. There is, it seems, an endless litany of what those other things that engage our minds are, when we should be intent, concentrated, and focused on what the other person is saying to us. What we do in our minds depends on who the other person is and our existing relationship to them, what they are talking about and how we already think and feel about the topic, and the degree of difference between speaker and listener—primary language, race, culture, age, even, or especially, political, economic, religious, or psychological approaches to the subject of our communication.

An additional reality underlies all communication. We just don't remember or absorb all the content of a conversation, no matter what the circumstances or the topic at hand. The researchers spoke of studies that show that after a ten-minute oral presentation, most people only retain about 50 percent of what they heard or what was said. Within forty-eight hours, that dropped off another 50 percent, so that only about 25 percent was remembered, let alone understood or comprehended.

As we grow older, we lose concentration and our ability to listen suffers. It begins very early. A study done with teachers in the Minneapolis schools, grades one through twelve, revealed startling and discouraging results. It was conducted by Ralph G. Nichols, a professor of rhetoric at the University of Minnesota (retired), and he shares his conclusions in his book *Are You Listening?*. The teachers would be speaking as they normally do, then stop abruptly and ask the students, "What was I talking about? What are you thinking about?" In the early grades, first and second, about 90 percent were paying attention and listening. But in each higher grade, the percentage dropped substantially until in junior high, only 44 percent were listening, and in high school classes, the average listening rate was down to 28 percent.

Eyes see only light. Ears hear only sound but a listening heart perceives meaning.
—David Steindl-Rast, *A Listening Heart*

Listening is hard. This is the place to begin. The act of listening demands that we pay attention and move outside ourselves, displace ourselves, and attend to another's voice, person, presence, and words with all our being. There are the words—the content—but there is the depth and breadth of meaning that is conveyed in tone of voice, timbre, pauses, hesitations, the rise and fall of loudness, whispers, sighs, and choked or impassioned intonation. I once heard the Dalai Lama speak about listening, and he described most of our listening as being like a container with holes. We're listening, but we're losing as much if not more than what we're retaining.

He called it lack of mindfulness and memory, and so we often don't benefit from what we hear or actually perceive what has been shared with us by another. Our interest can't be half-hearted. When we listen, it's not just for the points made or information shared or knowledge added to our own store, but the core, the heart of what is said; in some manner, it's a bit of the person speaking.

I am a storyteller, a theologian (the dubious practice of studying God!), and a preacher that tells portions of the Scriptures, the Judeo-Christian ones, some Buddhist sutras and koans, pieces of Native traditions, and poetry and tales from many cultural and religious traditions— and I tell them by heart. They are not memorized but absorbed and told with an underlying ear for their overall sense as well as specific words and phrases. I hear and listen to the texts as I speak them, and others hear and listen to them as well. Many educational theorists say that whatever enters the human body through your eyes goes straight to your head/your brain and whatever enters through your ears goes straight to your heart. Listening sensitizes that path from ears to heart, gathering layers of meaning and intent in the hard work of integrating another's meaning into your own.

Often when I first begin a class, I tell the students an old Jewish teaching story about the kind of students there are and which ones teachers hope for when they stand before others and teach.[3] This is the way I tell the story:

Once upon a time, there was a group of rabbis and they got to talking about the students in their classes and those that they found most difficult to deal with and those that they remembered from times past who made teaching so rich that they as teachers learned from them.

One rabbi began with the first group called funnels. "I speak and it goes in one ear and out the other. I look at them and there is no recognition that anything registered with them at all. When I ask for a response, even for them to just repeat what I said, there is a blank stare. Frustrating, again and again I feel like I'm speaking to a wall." Another rabbi said, "My hardest students are strainers. I speak and they listen, and what I say gathers in the strainer and anything of worth seems to seep right out and all that is left is sludge. I could pour a bottle of expensive wine into them, and all they'd keep is the lees and all that precious liquid is wasted. They love details, facts, interesting tidbits, but they are not into keeping anything of importance. Sad, so much is lost."

The next rabbi had been nodding in agreement and he added, "My group is like a sponge. They soak in everything and the sponge begins to be saturated and leak and drip. They get a lot of what I'm saying, but they do not absorb, or know when to squeeze and let some of it go, let alone respond or question or ask for clarification. Great possibilities but, in the end, we go nowhere together." The rabbi that had been silent during the conversation finally spoke: "I look for students that are like sieves. They can discern what is crucial and let all the dross or the insignificant material pass through the holes. They know how to sift, shake, and eliminate what is not helpful and keep the kernels that make for fine flours. They take what is needed first and then eventually, hopefully look at the dust and chaff, the coarse meal that they have discarded and begin to see what they might be useful for, because they are aware that there is meaning there—for meaning is in all things."

The rabbis decided that the ideal student is one who listens to the text they are studying and to the commentary of the teacher and the ideas of the other students, listening, sifting, adding their own feelings, knowledge, and experience and all the while, stands humbly before the others knowing that we all dwell in mystery. This is the student, the listener who is blessed and is a blessing upon all around them.

After a silence, one of the rabbis asked, "What about us? Which kind of student and listener are we?" It's a marvelous story describing many of our own ways of listening and not listening, whether we find ourselves in a classroom, or working with others, or listening to a talk, or engaged in a conversation with one person, or many.

To be a good listener is a gift—to everyone.

What a delight to be honored, described, and complimented as a superb listener! I read Richard Mabey's review of a book called *Findings* by Kathleen Jamie. This is the way he spoke of her: "Kathleen Jamie is a supreme listener...in the quietness of her listening, you hear her own voice, clear, subtle, respectful and so unquenchably curious that it makes the world anew." This is the act of listening translated onto paper and it has as much to do with seeing and remembering as it does with listening and integrating content into one's own person.

Many of my friends are friends with cats and dogs (and other creatures as well!), and I discovered the following gem in a book of pictures/cartoons and words called *Guardians of Being: Spiritual Teachings from Dogs and Cats.* It is sage advice for us two-leggeds, aka human beings.

> Give yourself completely to the act of listen-
> ing. Beyond the sounds there is something
> greater: a sacredness that cannot be under-
> stood through thought.[4]

Each person, each encounter, each conversation has this element of the sacred, and the art of listening is sensing that sacredness, honoring it and being humble and in awe before it—an atom of that person's essence and being. It's like trying to catch what is over, under, behind, beside, around, and in the person's words and voice, in layers under all the surfaces. This kind of listening has to become more than just a specific experience or a momentary act, it has to become a lifestyle, an attitude of being, and a receptivity toward and with others—all others. There is a saying from Ecuador: "To a good listener only a few words are needed." This kind of listening requires attentiveness and skill. It is the practice of the virtue of being humbled before another.

The power of listening is matched perhaps only by the power of the need and desire for each of us to be heard, to be listened to—with the ear of the heart and the openness of one who will attend to us. Decades ago, I was in the seminary and one of my closest friends there left after ordination. He took a number of jobs to live on while he decided what he was going to do with the rest of his life. One of those jobs was being a cabdriver in Washington, DC. We'd get together and catch up at least once a year over a long leisurely dinner and tell stories of what we'd experienced since we last met. One night, he was describing what it was like driving a cab in all areas of the city late at night. He'd pick up a stranger, find out where they wanted to go, and realize as he was driving that they wanted him to take the longest route to their destination, or sometimes they'd pay him just to drive around for an hour or more. They wanted to talk to someone—or more to the heart of the matter, they wanted someone to listen to them. So he'd drive and they would lean forward, close to the glass or plastic divider between the front and back seats, and begin to share the most incredible things with him.

In a word, they confessed to him—never knowing that had been and still was his original vocation. Sometimes, they'd even kneel on the hump in the floor and whisper into the opening in the partition. Once started, their confessions would come out in a flood of words, sometimes sobs of despair, of being lost, of need, and of wanting to be heard, listened to, accepted, and taken to heart—to be reassured that they were still someone, someone that mattered, that they were listened to and forgiven, that they were still human, and that their lives could go on. He said he was floored, humbled, amazed just listening. He rarely said anything when the stranger would begin to talk—only once in a while acknowledging that he was still there, present to them and listening. They talked of affairs, unfaithfulness, the need for their husband or wife, or friend or lover to pay attention to them. They spoke of corruption and stealing, fraud and business practices in their companies and personal lives. They spoke of choices they made that were disastrous and didn't know how to undo; they spoke of those they lost—still raw with grief—relatives, friends, and children they never had; and they spoke of fears of illness and loss of their jobs, their self-respect, and dying.

Inevitably would come a moment of silence. Then he would speak—reassuring them that he had heard what they were saying; he had listened to them. He would try in simple words to encourage them, to connect with them, and to give them hope so that they could continue living. When they would get to their destination and get out of the cab, they always, if only for a fleeting moment, looked him right in the eye and thanked him; some smiled; some were still crying. Some paid him, some forgot to! Some tipped him generously. He said he'd always drive away and feel as though he had been honored with an incredible gift of a person's life and all he had to do was just listen as long as they needed to talk. He said those were the nights that he learned what certain words that he'd picked up years previously meant. They were words from the beginning of the Rule of St. Benedict (a guide for a monastic community of men and women founded in the fourth century). The words were "Listen, my child with the ear of your heart."

His stories and words reminded me of the words of an amazing physician, Rachel Naomi Remen—a storyteller and author who teaches doctors and medical professionals to listen to their patients' stories, along with sharing diagnosis and treatment suggestions. She has said often in interviews, "When you listen generously to people, they can hear the truth in themselves, often for the first time." These words are one way of asking what meaning we are seeking to hear as we listen to people speaking to us. It is as much about what is not said, as what is articulated and what is hidden in all the aspects of speaking. This kind of listening means becoming vulnerable and opening yourself to whatever is shared. This is learning to open more deeply to the mystery of what it is to be a human being in communication with another human being. It is a moment that is as simple as a child attuned to their mother or father; as complex as understanding a scientific theory; as intense as accepting another person without trying to second-guess them, judge them, or react rather than respond to them; it is as freeing as literally releasing someone from slavery and bondage.

LISTEN: JUST LISTEN!

There are so many difficulties in just listening. So much in our nature and often in our cultures can hinder us from whole-hearted listening. We can get caught up in when and where we decide to listen; we can decide we have more important things to do; or we can find that what we are listening to is boring, we're not interested, or we decide in a hasty judgment that we don't care much for the person we'd have to listen to at that moment—or ever. We have no intention of actually listening—we're busy thinking/planning/emoting about what we are more concerned with at the moment. This is a story that has been told many times since it first happened almost ten years ago in Washington, DC, in January on a busy morning in a freezing Metro station. Thousands and thousands of people pass through the station—it being one of the cross-over points for other lines in the Metro system.

A young nondescript man was busking, as many performers do during rush hour, with his instrument case open in front of him for any donations and offerings. He was playing the violin. He played for an hour and played six pieces of music—all Bach. There were an estimated two thousand people who got off and on trains and passed right in front of him. Researchers kept tabs on who stopped to listen and who gave money during the hour's performance. After three minutes, a middle-aged man caught sight of him, slowed down, and then stopped for a few seconds, engrossed in listening. Then the man almost jerked as he pulled himself away and hurried on to wherever he was going. After four minutes, someone in passing dropped the first dollar bill in his case. Then another, a woman, dropped some coins that she had in her pocket into the case, but didn't stop or even look at him. After six minutes, a young man stopped, leaned against the wall and listened, getting into the music. But then he glanced at his watch and left. At ten minutes, a child about three or four years old stopped. He was entranced by the musician. He was holding onto his stroller while his mother pulled him along. They continued but he kept his head turned, watching and listening until the crowd obscured him.

This scenario was repeated a number of times—always women with young children. Not a one that wanted to stop and listen was allowed to—each was pulled away.

He played another forty-five minutes, engrossed in his music, yet still seeking to engage anyone who'd listen. In the end, only six people stopped and listened for any length of time. About twenty people gave him money but kept moving along. His take was thirty-two dollars. When his hour was over, he packed up his violin, took the money and the case, and left. There was silence once again in the Metro station except for the usual noise of a weekday morning crowd. No one ever applauded. There was no recognition. There was no connection to speak of.

The *Washington Post* had set this experiment up as part of a study on perception, taste, people's priorities, and what would make people stop and listen, specifically in a place where people wouldn't necessarily stop or expect to hear or listen to music and the musician. No one knew or noticed that the musician was Joshua Bell, one of the most acclaimed violinists in the world. He played six pieces of Bach, some of the most intricate pieces ever written, on a violin that was worth over 3.5 million dollars. Just two nights previously, he had played to a sold-out crowd in Boston where the tickets went for about a hundred dollars apiece. The *Post* asked the following questions: Why didn't people stop? Why didn't anyone listen? Even if they didn't appreciate classical music or realize who it was who was playing, why didn't they at least listen to such beauty, such obvious skill and passionate devotion? Then they asked: If we were missing out on that as we went about our lives, what else are we missing, not hearing, not paying attention to, not listening to, and not receiving as a gift? This story reveals how much an impact just the place and the environment as well as our prior intent and agendas can have on our listening—even to something of beauty, something that can enrich us and bring us pleasure, gracing our day. If this is the reality we find ourselves in, what do we not hear or refuse to listen to because it is difficult, unpleasant, hard, distasteful, annoying, upsetting, or would demand a response or change?

But listening can be learned. It is a practice, a discipline, a skill, and a consciousness that we can become aware of and improve. We have to begin by deciding that listening is more important perhaps than speaking. It is coming to the conclusion that the other's words are at least as crucial, if not more so, than our own. In Africa, there is a riddle: "Why do we have two ears and only one tongue?" Simple—every child singsongs the answer: "Because we have to listen twice as much and twice as hard as we talk!" This reflects the respect that is expected of children in that culture as well as of adults. This is very African in culture and value, and many of us in the West (and elsewhere) may not live this way!

Someone sent me a short, one-page reflection by a man who lived in Africa for more than twenty-five years but now lives in Sweden in the region of Norrland—as he describes it, a straddling existence, one foot in Mozambique and one foot in the western world in the far north. He tells a story that he overheard years ago that is steeped in the wisdom of sages and questions us at our roots. He was in Maputo in Mozambique and it was hot, probably easily over 100 degrees in the theater he had been rehearsing in with others. He fled outside and the only bench was already occupied by two old African men. But, as he says, "There was room for me too. In Africa, people share more than just water in a brotherly or sisterly fashion. When it comes to shade, people are generous." He sat there, content not to move, and he heard the two men talking about a third man, a friend who had recently died. Then he started listening closely. This is what he wrote:

> One of them said, "I was visiting him in his home. He started to tell me an amazing story about something that had happened to him when he was young. But it was a long story. Night came, and we decided that I should come back the next day to hear the rest. But when I arrived, he was dead."
>
> The man fell silent. I decided not to leave that bench until I heard how the other man would respond to what he'd heard. I had an instinctive feeling that it would prove to be important.
>
> Finally he, too, spoke.
>
> "That's not a good way to die—before you've told the end of your story."
>
> It struck me as I listened to those two men that a truer nomination for our species than *Homo sapiens* might be *Homo narrans*, the storytelling person. What differentiates us from

animals is the fact that we can listen to other people's dreams, fears, joys, sorrows, desires, and defeats—and they in turn can listen to ours.[5]

What a story! What wisdom! These men were sages in the truest sense of the word. In Latin, the word for sage—*sapere*—means "to taste," from the noun *sap*, meaning "taste." Originally a verb, being *sage* is an attitude gleaned from experiences, narratives shared, gestures seen and repeated, a lifestyle of imbibing, of tasting the richness and diversity of others' lives where we have been invited into others' worlds. It is born of listening!

There will be many stories in this book, because listening to people is most often listening to their stories at a moment in time and place. We cross paths with people, sometimes we stay awhile, sometimes we linger as long as we can. Sometimes we decide to stay and listen and live in various relationships of being together and impacting one another's lives. When we hear, there is always information, knowledge, data, but there is also the listening and catching the mystery, the heart and the essence of the person speaking with/to us and our replies, reactions, responses that they hear and listen to.

We can learn a great deal about listening by hearing and listening to texts: those written down and commented upon and those found in the oral traditions of the religions of the world, as well as in stories, parables, poems, and prayers. We can learn to listen in situations of public talks, teachers' lectures, the media of the DVD, CD, public radio, cinema, and even books on tape. All of these are excellent practice for listening to human beings' voices and to those who stand in our presence as we stand in their presence.

To bring this section to a close and to segue into the next section on listening to texts, specifically religious ones in various traditions, especially those of the People of the Book—Judaism, Christianity, and Islam—there is another story. I heard this told at an interreligious dialogue conference, and I've been told that a version appears in a collection, *The Essential Jewish Stories—Torah*, in the section on Students and Teachers. This is how I remember hearing it and listening intrigued, wanting to listen like the young female student in the story. I distinctly remember her name, Laura. I don't remember the teacher's! And I don't remember the names of the schools.

The teacher tells it from his point of view. He began to speak of a young female student who had been accepted at a rabbinic school. She was in the seminary and on occasions she would drop into his office and they would talk. Once when she visited, it was she who told him the story. It was in her senior year, and one of her professors who had gotten to know her a bit asked her, "Laura, how do you think you're going to do on my exam in a couple of days?" She smiled at him and said, "I'm looking forward to it—I think I know exactly what you're going to ask. You always have ten questions, so I studied and took notes keeping that in mind and I think I've figured out which ten questions are on the exam." The professor was intrigued and said, "OK, try me. Tell me the ten questions on the exam." And she did! She told him the ten questions very close to how they would be phrased, and in the order they were asked! He was stunned and dismayed.

He didn't want to believe it, but it was obvious that she had somehow gotten hold of the exam, copied it, and knew what to answer. He began to worry—had she hacked into his computer or gotten into his office? Had she shared the questions with other students? She shook her head and denied any wrongdoing. She told him bluntly, "I know you. I know how you teach, and I pay close attention and listen carefully to what you emphasize and I take notes." But the dean was brought in and after listening to the professor's concerns, asked her, "Do you know the questions?" She answered truthfully and said, "Yes, I do. I was at all the lectures. I listened and took careful notes." His response was, "I'm sure you did—and I'm sure many other students did the same. But you even know the order, as you stated, that the questions will be asked. Unless you can prove otherwise, you cannot take the exam, and you will be barred from graduation and, of course, from being ordained. This school does not countenance dishonesty—especially when it is so brazen and arrogant."

But she was not upset. She calmly said, "I can prove that I did not cheat or steal anything. There is a notebook in my desk and in it are the notes I took in the class. If you look back through the notes you will see stars placed next to specific texts and commentaries and statements of the professor. Some have one or two stars...some more, but there are only ten segments that have seven stars—stars of David next to them. That is the material and they contain the questions in the order they will be asked. That's what I've studied since the professor emphasized them so repeatedly—even as he summarized the class in the last session." The notebook was retrieved by the professor who came back reading it and was stunned. It was just as she has said. Extensive notes, with various stars of David—up to the number seven, and the segments marked with seven stars were the material that formed his questions. The segments were marked numerically but out of sequence—one through ten. Both of them were at a loss for words.

Finally, her professor spoke, saying, "You did listen to me, more than anyone has ever listened to me before in a class. You listened and heard what I was trying to say that was important and you sensed the internal dynamics of the material. Then you listened and could anticipate what I'd shared and what I wanted you to think was essential." The dean suggested that it was not necessary for her to take the final exam. Afterward, her professor wondered, "If she could hear and listen to my thoughts so closely, did she also listen and sense who I am and what is essential in my life as a rabbi?"

She went on to become a rabbi—when the story was told, we spoke about it in small groups afterward. People had trouble believing that it actually happened and that she was that good at listening and sensing, knowing the professor. I heard the story and what he had said about her—accused her of, intending to stop her graduation and ordination, and wondered if he asked himself how well he listened to his students or had listened to her when she stopped by to see him on occasion in his office.

I wondered what she felt as she listened to him and what he assumed about her, missing anything of her truthfulness and integrity during the classes she took with him. Nothing about that was said. But in the small group, someone reflected after I mentioned it: "I hope I can find someone who listens to me like that." Another said, "And I hope that I can listen like that to everyone."

This listening involves listening to words and thoughts for content; listening to the words of peoples' souls and hearts and experiences. When we listen to the Word (oral and written), we find the whole person, a person living within their tradition and within the accumulated listening of generations. *Listen Here!*

REFLECTIONS AND PRACTICES

1. The opening story speaks about four kinds of students —or listeners. They are the funnel, the strainer, the sponge, and the sieve. Which one, would you say, you are? When you talk with other people, is there one kind of listener that you feel is listening to you?

2. There is a Turkish saying: "To speak is to sow; to listen is to reap." Is there a person in your life that, when you listen to them, you feel like you are always reaping—harvesting wisdom? Are you aware of listening to that person differently than others? How would you describe what your relationship is to that person—before they even speak?

3. People in the story of Joshua Bell were intent on doing something else, going somewhere, aware of

time, and had their own priorities when they passed him by. Reflect on your daily routines. Are you conscious of times and places when you are so intent on what you're already doing that you don't hear anyone or anything else?

3

LISTENING TO THE TEXTS

Every word and every being come knocking at your door, bringing you their mystery. If you are open to them, they will flood you with their riches.

—Irenee Guilane Dioh

Poetry must not perish. Otherwise, what hope for the world?

—Leopold Sedar Senghor

When peaceful silence lay over all, and night had half run her swift course, Your all-powerful Word leapt down from Heaven.

—Wisdom 18:14–15

*Now in the deep womb of the Sacred Word I
will search for myself in Spirit and in Truth.*
                            —St. Bernard of Clairvaux

In many countries where I have traveled, I have heard a statement that each particular people of differing beliefs and practices in their respective religious traditions claims as their own. It is short and simple and provocative for some. It is the following: "Whatever name you call God by, God's name is Truth." Many countries embrace a particular religion as their national or state religion. During World War II, the emperor of Japan declared war on the United States and the document sounds like a religious declaration. The people of Japan were encouraged to pray to their gods/buddhas (*shinbutsu*) for victory and to invoke the help of their ancestors.

In the United States, in practically every Presidential State of the Union Address or other official speech, whether appealing to the citizens of the United States for votes or explaining a political or economic decision, even minor politicians end their discourse with these words: "God bless America." Lately, in many of the speeches and decrees of the Kremlin in Russia, the leader likewise ends with invoking the gods of Russian Orthodoxy. It seems that many of these gods are very parochial, tribal, nationalistic rather than universal, as the line about God being Truth asserts. It might be said another way: What language (or languages) does God speak? Most people would readily say that God speaks, hears, listens to, and understands all languages. But unfortunately human beings only speak and understand and listen in a few languages. Anyone who speaks fluently even one or two languages realizes that what one says and what one hears and understands in another language—even the same idea or concept, transliterated word for word—knows the gaps and differences in speaking and listening. This is not only true in common discourse and communication between people, but it is true in the theological languages of religion. It appears that God breaks and crosses over boundaries among people, universally on earth (and perhaps in the heavens too!).

Each of the major religions has its own sacred text, scriptures both oral and written that reveal a god-language, a perception of reality, a stance in the world, ethics, spirituality, and a sense of what it means to be a human being in relationship to the holy, to all others, and to the earth, all creation. The texts are psalms/poems and prayers, stories, histories, exhortations, laments, teachings, instructions for discipline, meditation practices, public rites, rituals, and worship. There are the three religions of the Book: Judaism, Christianity, and Islam. Then there is Buddhism, Hinduism, Confucianism, and all the religions of native peoples. There are, of course, many other sects and denominations within all these religions. When we look at all the religions, and read/hear and listen to their writings, texts, and stories that are the sources of their wisdom, practice, prayer, and worship, what becomes immediately apparent is the vastness of God, the spaciousness of God, the power of God that is both singularly personal and communally

bonding, and is vibrantly alive in both historical tradition and contemporary reality. Max Muller, a scholarly
pioneer of comparative religion, said, "He who knows
one [religion], knows none."[1] Each religion, all religions,
have a broad spectrum of believers and practitioners as
well as an extensive coda of beliefs and commentaries—
responses to the originating traditions over the centuries. People confess and follow a religion because they
feel that this way of looking at truth and living with
integrity is what will make them most human—and
adherents of every religion believe that their religion is
the true religion. But it is "true" with a small *t* whereas
God is Truth that is universally encompassing and larger
and more mysterious, more God than any religion or
any expression of belief.

There is a saying among storytellers: "There is only
one Story, how do you tell it?" Each and every person,
no matter their faith, can begin to answer by referring
to their own heritage, tradition, and sources of wisdom
and knowledge. In a world that is growing smaller with
the advent and development of electronic, digital, and
instantaneous communication, it is imperative that no
matter which religion we practice as believers, we must
be aware of, know about, and listen to the faith and
understandings of other religions and other peoples'
beliefs. That is perhaps most easily accessible by hearing, listening to, and seeking understanding in stories
and sacred texts from religious traditions and coming to
appreciate the treasures found in the wisdom of each of
the world traditions. Each religion passes on acquired

experience of what is holy, how to relate to God, and how to be human.

Perhaps we should begin with a story from Islam:

Once upon a time, the Prophet, Mohammed, was making a pilgrimage to one of the holy cities and the day had been long. He looked and found a tree that would give some shelter for the night and, after saying his prayers, took his cloak, rolled himself in it against the chill, and slept. But very early in the morning, while it was still dark, he was rudely shaken awake by another group of pilgrims who were incensed at him. It took a moment for him to awake and listen to what they were saying. It seems that in the dark, when he chose his spot to rest, he didn't have his feet pointing toward Allah, toward Mecca. He was a bit stunned by their anger and insistence, so he immediately put his feet in the right direction. Then he spoke: "There is no place where Allah is not!" He pulled his cloak around himself again and laid back down and went to sleep.

This echoes many other religious traditions—"If you can't find God in this place [a difficult one, or a destroyed city or in the midst of violence and hate] you will not find God in anyplace" (Christian tradition). God is everywhere and there is no place where God is not. Anthony de Mello, a Catholic Jesuit spiritual teacher, once told a Hindu story that religion is a finger pointed at the moon. The intent is to leap from the end of the finger to the moon—but often we get stuck on the finger! We become more interested in whose finger it is, its color and hue, whether it belongs to a man or a woman, young person or old person, a priest or "ordinary" person, if it has a ring on it, even which finger it is! But it's the moon that is the endpoint. It can be argued this is true in all religions.

We all have to be careful that we don't make our God in our image. Instead, the power of God is that each of us and all of us are made in God's image, and our behaviors and practice of our chosen religion reveals to others who our God is, what is the essence of our God, and how we worship and imitate God. Meister Eckhart, a thirteenth-century German mystic (at some points in his life considered a heretic and dangerous), once said, "Whoever seeks God in a special way gets the way and misses God." A surprising comment, much like a Buddhist koan or a parable of Jesus.

At its root, every religion is a way of listening to God and listening to one's own soul, listening to others' hearts, even listening to all the universe for truth that is universal and yet specific to each of us. In the First Book of Samuel, there is the story of Eli, who is the priest at Shiloh about three-thousand years ago, and one of his young assistants, Samuel. Samuel is born to Hannah who has been barren, and she gives her child to God when he graciously gives her a child. Eli is growing old and Samuel relies on him. The story is telling about a number of things and it begins with listening.

> The boy Samuel ministered before the LORD under Eli. In those days the word of the LORD was rare; there were not many visions.
>
> One night Eli, whose eyes were becoming so weak that he could barely see, was lying down in his usual place. The lamp of God had not yet

gone out, and Samuel was lying down in the temple of the LORD, where the ark of God was. Then the LORD called Samuel.

Samuel answered, "Here I am." And he ran to Eli and said, "Here I am: you called me."

But Eli said, "I did not call: go back and lie down." So he went and lay down.

Again the LORD called, "Samuel!" And Samuel got up and went to Eli and said, "Here I am: you called me."

"My son," Eli said. "I did not call; go back and lie down."

Now Samuel did not yet know the LORD. The word of the LORD had not yet been revealed to him.

The LORD called Samuel a third time, and Samuel got up and went to Eli and said, "Here I am: you called me."

Then Eli realized that the LORD was calling the boy. So Eli told Samuel, "Go and lie down and if he calls you say: 'Speak, Lord, for your servant is listening.' So Samuel went and lay down in his place.

The LORD came and stood there, calling as at the other times, "Samuel! Samuel!"

Then Samuel said, "Speak, for your servant is listening."

And the LORD said to Samuel, "See, I am about to do something in Israel that will make the ears of everyone who hears of it tingle. (1 Sam 3:1–11)

The story has become the classic invitation that God is the initiator in any conversation and relationship, though each person needs others to give them insight and begin to help them on their journey. It is in listening—a listening that is repeated, listening that can come at any hour of the day or night, and to the least likely person, not the one you might think would be the one to receive the Word of the Lord. One of the ways each person in their tradition hears the Word and begins to listen to the presence and will of God is found in these stories of the tradition—of those who have gone before us and their experience—and becomes a model of our own experience and knowledge. When Samuel gets up in the morning and tells Eli what the Lord has shared with him, it is not easy news. It is a shift in how the Lord deals with Israel as a nation and who the Lord chooses to speak to, and to speak for God to the people. But Samuel tells Eli everything he has heard and listened to in the night. And we are told as the story's ending what Samuel's life is like after listening to the Lord.

> The LORD was with Samuel as he grew up, and he let none of his words fall to the ground. And all Israel from Dan to Beersheba recognized that Samuel was attested as a prophet of the LORD. The LORD continued to appear at Shiloh, and there he revealed himself to Samuel through his word. And Samuel's word came to all Israel. (1 Sam 3:19—4:1a)

In many of the stories and accounts, in much of the revelation of religion, the one who listens and can hear the Word of the Lord hears on behalf of the people. The one who is the prophet, the hearer and repeater of the words of God, becomes like a tuning fork—attentive to any slight shift in sound, silence, and often music—to hear and listen and understand what he hears and then pass it on to others. It is not given to them primarily as an individual, but given to give away to the people. God and the Word of God can come at any moment, anywhere, to anyone—but it all begins with listening. Then it becomes a spoken word for others to listen to. This act of listening, hearing, speaking, and sharing sound that is insightful and powerful is a sacred act.

> *Why is the spoken word so special? Its function is to evoke the breath of the Supreme Being, of his omnipotence. It is the ideal vehicle of the divine, of cosmic energy.*
> —Alassane Ndaw

The sound of the Word of God, the sound of God, comes through human voices and so the act of listening, the act of speaking, and the act of transmittal truthfully is holy, and is as much a part of worship and teaching as the other forms of ritual that involve objects, rites, and an order that is observed. Perhaps the most sacred and one of the most important pieces of the earlier testament of Judaism is what is called the Shema. There are six verses in the first section found in Deuteronomy 6:4–9,

the second section are the verses of Deuteronomy
11:13–21, and the third section is found in Numbers
15:37–41. Together these verses comprise the twenty
verses that every Jew is obligated to recite each morning and evening of their lives. They remind the Jewish
people of the fundamental beliefs and practices that
constitute being a Jew. They are the oneness of God, our
love for God, the study of Torah; education, the
mitzvoth of *tefillin*, *mezuzah*, and *tzitzit*; and the concept of reward and punishment and the remembrance of
the Exodus. This is how it reads:

> Hear, O Israel, the L-rd our G-d, the L-rd is One.
> You shall love the L-rd your G-d with all your
> heart, with all your soul and with all your
> might. These words, which I command you this
> day shall be upon your heart; you shall teach
> them thoroughly to your children, and you
> shall speak of them when sitting in your home
> and walking on the road, when you lie down
> and when you arise. You shall bind them as a
> sign upon your hand and they shall be as
> *tefillin* between your eyes. You shall write them
> on your doorposts of your home and gates.

This imperative to "Hear, O Israel" in this first segment is singular in intent as a command to obey. In the
second segment found in Deuteronomy 11:13–17, the
command is repeated, but now it is in the plural—with
"all your hearts and all your souls"—it is an imperative

to the whole people. One of the teachings of the Lubavitcher Rebbe explains succinctly what this means.

> Our connection with G-d is realized by two general means: our study of Torah and our observance of the mitzvoth. Torah is our experience of G-d. Torah is what G-d revealed of Himself to us allowing us a glimpse of His wisdom and a glimmer of insight into the essence of His creation and His relationship with us....In building our relationship from the bottom up deed precedes experience: first must come a firm grounding, our commitment, upon which can be based the more intellectual aspects of the relationship....concrete action precedes Torah.[2]

The text itself (or the story, parable, koan, teaching) is holy and to be repeated/prayed/chanted aloud and to be heard by others, listened to, and appropriated. But the commentaries and stories about the stories and texts are sacred too. Together they form a bond. It is said that the Torah, the Law, was given to the people through Moses by day, but at night, God spoke in midrash, stories and examples to all. Here is one of the famous commentaries on the Shema:

> A disciple asks his rebbe, "Why does Torah tell us to 'place these words UPON your hearts'? Why does it not tell us to place these holy words IN our hearts?" The rebbe answers, "It is because as we are, our hearts are closed, and we cannot place the holy words in our hearts.

So we place them on top of our hearts. And there they stay until, one day, the heart breaks and the words fall in."[3]

THE SOUND OF THE WORD/THE STORY

In the midst of an interreligious dialogue in Detroit a few years ago, a young woman imam passed me a handwritten note. I had finished telling stories from the Qur'an, the earlier testament of the Jewish people, and the Gospel of Matthew. I do not know where it comes from....I only have her words:

The sound of a story "in the world is important." Sound and meaning are largely inseparable. As God's creative word (Gen 1; Isa 55:10–11) now reverberates through the cosmos. The meaning is implicit though humans don't necessarily hear, heed, or respond in wonder, the meaning still resounds, a numinous vibrato. Conversion presupposes turning into intrinsic truth. Our lack of listening doesn't diminish the word's integrity—only ours suffer.

When I had read the note and looked up, she was smiling at me, mouthing the words "Keep telling—someone is listening; someone needs to hear." Her words echo in my heart. I hope I have heeded them. This reality of the sound of the teacher, the storyteller, the believer is shared by other traditions. This is how the followers of Buddha speak to the concept:

*We are no longer able to hear the Buddha's
voice. However, we can still hear voices that
come close to his. When all things of this
world that have a voice together raise their
voices, retaining their individual character
yet combining them in one large sound,
then we are very, very close to the sound of
the Buddha's voice.*
—Kukai, *The Principles of Sound, Meaning
and Reality* (Shoji-jisso-gi)

OBEDIENCE

In the language of Latin, the primary meaning of the verb *to listen* is "to obey"! In fact, the verbs that we translate into English as "to hear," "to believe," and "to act upon" are all the same in a number of languages. We can separate out the concepts and even the actions in the Western world, but in the Middle Eastern world and at the time of Jesus, they are/were intimately and strongly connected together as one. To hear (to actually listen) is to believe, and to believe is to understand so that you act. In many Western languages and cultures, you can hear something and not believe it; you can believe it and not practice or act upon that belief; you can act upon what is commanded but not have heard, and so on. But for many earlier languages, they are all of a piece, united.

But what does the word *obey* mean? We might start by noting that the meaning of *hear* and *obey* in the Hebrew Scriptures is so close that the two can scarcely be separated. It is the implication of every "hear and obey" command of the Old Testament that unless the people of Israel were prepared to act upon the divine Word, they could not truly be said to have heard it. Even the Latin roots of the word *obedience* maintain this intimate connection; it is derived from the words meaning "toward" and "to hear," suggesting movement toward the truth one hears.

> Authentic obedience then has little to do with forced submission to a controlling and restrictive authority. It has much to do with attunement to the truth of one's source and end. To follow the deepest structure and potential of one's created being is obedience to truth and results not in a sense of imposed constriction but in joyful fulfillment.[4]

This understanding of listening is profound and can be disturbing, too. This changes the way we hear many of the texts of the four Gospels and many other sacred writings. Perhaps one of the most definitive of Jesus' messages and mission and what he believed, practiced, taught, and lived—and died for—is found in Luke. It is called the reason for Jesus' being baptized—and so all those who believe in him being baptized; his political, economic, and religious agenda, personally and for his communities; and his beginning of the proclamation of the good news to the poor.

> Jesus returned to Galilee in the power of the Spirit, and news about him spread through the

whole countryside. He taught in their syna-
gogues, and everyone praised him. He went to
Nazareth, where he had been brought up, and
on the Sabbath day he went to the synagogue
as was his custom. And he stood up to read.
The scroll of the prophet Isaiah was handed to
him. Unrolling it, he found the place where it
is written:

"The Spirit of the Lord is upon me, because
he has anointed me to preach good news to the
poor, He has sent me to proclaim freedom for
the prisoners and recovery of sight to the
blind, to release the oppressed, and to proclaim
a year of the Lord's favor."

Then he rolled up the scroll, gave it back to
the attendant and sat down. The eyes of everyone in the synagogue were fixed on him, and he
began by saying to them: "Today this scripture
is fulfilled in your hearing." (Luke 4:14–21)

Every translation, even this one, ends the text
poorly expressed; every English teacher would exclaim,
"You never end a sentence with a gerund!" The last line
should read, "Today this scripture passage is fulfilled
when you hear it!" That is a staggering statement,
provocative, demanding, filled with the call to obedience and pressure to obey! The only thing that stops the
words from becoming actuality, becoming true, is that
they, Jesus' audience in his hometown synagogue, do
not hear and so do not believe and so do not act upon
the belief and Jesus' words! Once we listen, we must

obey; not to obey says that we refuse to listen! In fact, in all the Scripture passages, to "be deaf" is to refuse to listen and so refuse to accept the words/teaching of Jesus, and in essence to refuse to believe and/or to follow Jesus. Jesus himself follows the ancient and universal command as he journeys to Jerusalem, lives, and dies because of his obedience to God to speak the Word and to live the Truth. In Jesus, Christians are called to hear, to listen, and to follow. This is how it is interpreted recently in a book published for believers to make their Lent more closely in imitation of Jesus:

> The word "obedience" means to "listen deeply." We know that to listen deeply requires the loss of ourselves, to forget ourselves. It means allowing the voice of the other to be heard. This is the beginning of humility. Jesus listened deeply to God within his heart and he was able to accept what God had asked of him, to allow himself to be lifted up so that he could draw all things to himself.[5]

With this understanding of "to listen" as "to obey," it becomes immediately apparent that who we listen to becomes the energizing force for our actions, our lives, and what drives our own decision-making and relationships with others in all areas of our lives—in a word—our *religion*. The word *religion* means "to tie or to bind together" much like the sinews, muscles, nerves, and fibers wrapped around bones/joints hold and bind the joints together and allow them to flex and move as well as to remain rigid and upright. Religion binds all areas of our lives together within the penetrating listening of our ears, our hearts, and our wills. In Middle Eastern thought even today, the heart is where our will is found and so to love with all our heart is to will with all the fibers of our being to do what we are commanded to do in response to what we hear and the words we listen to over and over again in times of reflection, prayer, ritual, and worship alone and with the rest of our community. And it is the others—our community that listens together to the Word of God—that hold us accountable to live with the integrity of our ears, hearts, wills, and minds. We listen together and struggle together to absorb and integrate, incarnate what we speak with our lips, hear with our ears, listen and treasure in our hearts and wills.

These stories, these texts, have inherent power, and power in the voices of those who speak/tell them and power in those who listen, in the communities and persons seeking wisdom. It is a threefold power, interpretation, and if you will, inspiration that operates in this shared listening to wisdom. Someone once said, "There is only one mountain, but many paths up." So many traditions follow the same climb, the same enduring struggle, but the particulars may alter. Rabbi Shlomo ibn Gabirol explained the overall process this way: "In seeking wisdom, the first step is silence, the second listening, the third remembering, the fourth practicing, and the fifth teaching others."

There are confusing wisdom stories, like some found among the Buddha's teachings that seek to share this wisdom:

Once upon a time, Buddha was growing old and he wanted to visit his communities one more time and share his last words and poems with them. It was a long and arduous trip around the mountain to the far communities, and only about three days and nights over the mountain. Though many of his followers told him not to go because the mountains were infested with bandits, he went anyway. He traveled for a day and a night (sleeping rough outside), and on the second day around noon, he stopped to rest and to meditate. He was feeling his age—and his weight. He had become rotund (much like many of the statues of the jolly roly-poly Buddha of today). It was a warm day and so he took off his shirt, stripped to the waist and sat under a tree, gathering himself, sitting in the lotus position with his hands folded. He was there for a while.

Then in the back of his mind, he heard the sound of horses' hooves pounding toward him over a wooden bridge that was nearby. He knew the horse was fully armed for battle and carried a rider fully armed from the sound and weight of the horse's tread. The rider, a warrior, pulled his horse to a halt just feet from Buddha on the ground. He threw his visor up and looked at him and started to roar with laughter. Buddha opened one eye and looked at him. After the man finished his laughter, he said to Buddha, "Do you know what you look like?" (Buddha didn't say anything.) "You look just like a pig!" He laughed again. Buddha opened both his eyes and looked at the warrior and said, "Do you know what you look like?" (He wasn't expecting any answer!) "Uh, no..." "You look just like God!" The warrior was dumbfounded. "What? I look like God? Is it my warrior's mien, my regal posture?" "No." "Is it my obvious power and arms?" "No." "Is it my wealth and position?" "No." "What is it then?" The Buddha looked at him and said very strongly. "I'm known to spend a lot of time looking for God, and after a while, everyone begins to look like God!" (And then reflectively to himself but so the warrior could hear very clearly, he said under his breath, "Hmm, I wonder what you spend a lot of time looking for?")

When this story is told, the effect is stunning—hearing it, listening with an open heart, and not expecting what is coming jars the mind and shatters the heart, and one must respond to the sound of it as it drops like a stone in your soul. These gems of stories and texts are found in every religion.

> *But what is amazing is that they are found not just in religious people, or texts, they are found in just about anyone anywhere!*
> *Every word and every being come knocking at your door, bringing you their mystery. If you are open to them, they will flood you with their riches.*
>
> —Irenee Guilane Dioh

What is found in the religions of the world, in their sacred words and texts can be touched, heard, sounded out, and experienced in the voices of people—wisdom can be stumbled over, bumped into, sidled up to, leaned against, overheard, and called forth. It is another way of listening—listening underneath what is apparent; listening and sensing—like pauses in a musical piece, learning that those rests, sighs are as critical as the notes themselves.

REFLECTIONS AND PRACTICES

1. Using one of the prayers, stories, or quotes in this chapter from a religion other than your own, spend some time reflecting and praying in light of that tradition.

2. Plan on studying with some depth the basic concepts and theology of one of the religions of the Book, or Buddhism, to recognize where your practice and belief connects, overlaps, or is in harmony with another religion.

3. If you are Christian/Catholic, try reading one Gospel through at one sitting. The Gospel of Mark only takes about fifteen minutes to read. Then read it once a week for a month and see what you learn/notice and begin to realize from your repeated reading. For Jews and Christians, the Book of Psalms is a place to begin together to reflect on being human, religious, and connected to all others and the earth. Good ones to begin with: Psalms 23, 29, 46, 113, 130, and 139.

4. To begin to look at an understanding of Islam, begin with some of the hundred names of Allah, such as

Allah The Greatest Name, Ar-Rahman The All Merciful, As-Salam The Source of Peace, Al-Ghaffar The Forgiving, Al-'Adl The Just, Ash-Shahid The Witness, Al-Haqq The Truth. To see a list of all the names, see *The Spiritual Gems of Islam*, as listed in the bibliography below.

AN INTRODUCTORY BIBLIOGRAPHY FOR SOME OF THE MAJOR RELIGIONS OF THE WORLD

JUDAISM

Buber, Martin. *I and Thou*. New York: Charles Scribner's Sons, 1970.

Gottlieb, Rabbi Lynn. *Trail Guide to the Torah of Nonviolence*. Paris: Editions Terre d'Esperance (Earth of Hope Publishing), 2013.

Heschel, Abraham Joshua. *Quest for God: Studies in Prayer and Symbolism*. New York: Crossroads, 1986.

Kushner, Lawrence. *The River of Light: Spirituality, Judaism, Consciousness*. Woodstock, VT: Jewish Lights, 1990.

Remen, Rachel Naomi. *Kitchen Table Wisdom: Stories that Heal*. New York: Riverhead, 1993.

Any books by Rabbi Zalman Schachter-Shalomi, Rabbi Rami Shapiro, and (for children) Sandy Eisenberg Sasso.

BUDDHISM

Aoyama, Shundo. *Zen Seeds: Reflections of a Female Priest*. Tokyo: Kosei, 1996.

Eppsteiner, Fred, ed. *The Path of Compassion: Writings on Socially Engaged Buddhism.* Berkeley, CA: Parallax, 1985.

His Holiness The Dalai Lama and Jean-Claude Carriere. *Violence and Compassion.* New York: Doubleday, 1994.

MacInnes, Elaine. *Zen Contemplation for Christians.* Lanham, MD: Rowman & Littlefield, 2003.

Nhat Hanh, Thich. *Being Peace.* Berkeley, CA: Parallax, 1987.

Any book by these writers and Joanna Macy, Robert Aitken, Robert Thurman, Pema Chodron. See Shambhala Publications, Inc., Boston, for other books.

CHRISTIANITY/CATHOLICISM

Bianchi, Enzo. *Words of Spirituality: Towards a Lexicon of the Inner Life.* London: SPCK, 2002.

Brueggemann, Walter. *Reality, Grief, Hope: Three Urgent Prophetic Tasks.* Grand Rapids: Eerdmans, 2014.

Gutierrez, Gustavo. *We Drink from Our Own Wells: The Spiritual Journey of a People.* Maryknoll, NY: Orbis, 1986.

Radcliffe, Timothy. *What Is the Point of Being Christian?* London: Burns and Oates, 2005.

Schori, Katharine Jefferts. *Gathering at God's Table: The Meaning of Mission in the Feast of Faith.* Woodstock, VT: Skylight Path, 2012.

Soelle, Dorothee. *Suffering.* Philadelphia: Fortress, 1975.

Williams, Rowan. *Where God Happens: Discovering Christ in One Another.* Boston: New Seeds, 2005.

Any books by these writers, and Leonard Boff, Dorothy Day, Thomas Merton, Desmond Tutu, and Jean Vanier.

ISLAM

Armstrong, Karen. *Islam: A Short History*. Modern Library. New York: Chronicle, 2000.

Dhondy, Farrukh. *Rumi: A New Translation of Selected Poems*. New York: Arcade Publishing, 2011.

Lefebure, Leo D. *True and Holy: Christian Scripture and Other Religions*. Maryknoll, NY: Orbis, 2014.

Rahman, Imam Jamal. *Spiritual Gems of Islam: Insights & Practices from the Qur'an, Hadith, Rumi and Muslim Teaching Stories to Enlighten the Heart and Mind*. Woodstock, VT: Skylight Paths, 2014.

Rahman, Jamal, Kathleen Schmitt Elias, and Ann Holmes Redding. *Out of Darkness into Light: Spiritual Guidance in the Quran with Reflections from Christian and Jewish Sources*. Harrisburg, NY: Morehouse, 2009.

Schwartz, Stephen. *The Other Islam: Sufism and the Road to Global Harmony*. New York: Doubleday, 2008.

(These books all have excellent bibliographies for further reading.)

4

FROM HEART-TO-HEART TO SOUL-TO-SOUL

It is important to learn how to listen with compassion. Listening with compassion means listening with the will to relieve others of their suffering, without judging or seeking to argue.

—Thich Nhat Hanh

We all exist solely for this—to be the human place God has chosen for his presence, his manifestation, his epiphany...we are God's words, we echo him, we signify and confirm him.

—Thomas Merton

These words are a good place to begin—if this is who each of us is in reality, then how do we listen to one another so that we can catch sight of (hear) and begin to sense who every person we meet actually is and what they might be trying to express, not just with their lives, but with their words day-to-day and their presence when they are with us? We have sought to listen to the words of other religions with the ear of the heart—or heart-to-heart. Now we will try to switch this power and skill to listening to others heart-to-heart. This means being present—being "there" with focus and concentration, open, vulnerable and receptive to another, open even to change; to being present with intent, intimacy, and acceptance, with equality, honoring the presence of the other. Listening with the heart—where our will is found—means listening and hoping, willing the fullness of life for another.

In the Gospels, this is the meaning of why the Word Jesus—God—became flesh (the mystery of the incarnation). In John's Gospel, Jesus says, "I have come that you might have life, life ever more abundantly" (10:10). This kind of listening begins with love—the openness to a relationship of intending and desiring the fullness of life for another, for all others who come into our presence and share time and space with us. It has been said that the first duty of love is to listen. When we listen with love, heart-to-heart, we understand not only what is said—its content—but we hear underneath, we stand under the one speaking and listen to their feelings, what is not being said, to their desires and fears; we sense their need and accept them; we know their weaknesses and strengths; we seek to sync our hearts together. This is a listening that demands that we step outside ourselves so that we make room for another person.

It will be stories that can give us a sense of what this is like—to experience and begin to understand the myriad ways listening can be expressed, known, and practiced. Let's go back to the beginnings of our lives—a very good place to start! Before we learned to speak, we made noises, sounds, picking up bits and pieces of speech from our parents and those who cared for us. (On occasion, adults find themselves reverting back to incoherent syllables, repeating what the infant is trying to say that sounds meaningless.) And yet, most parents and even older siblings and those who spend time and presence with infants understand something of the unintelligible gibberish that comes out of the infant and young child's mouth. When a baby cries, there are some who know what it wants and needs and is trying to indicate and share, but that is also the reality when it is just nonsense; that is the way we begin to communicate with others.

Among adults, it can happen too—if people are open and receptive to one another, approaching one another with respect, dignity, and freedom to mutually share the truth of the other. There is a great story told about Pope John XXIII soon after he was elected. He was due to meet with representatives of six European nations (EURATOM) to discuss the development of peaceful uses of atomic energy. The night before the meeting, Monsignor Capovilla, who had studied the issues scientifically, economically, and ethically, sought to explain in simple language to the pope what the situations entailed, some of the weightier ethical issues and what was involved with some basic scientific theories. He was hopeful that the pope would be able to participate more knowledgeably with the others at the meeting.

The meeting was going well until one of the representatives began to explain some of the technical, logistical, and scientific realities in great detail, way beyond the understanding of the pope and even some of the members of the group. It continued for a long time, until the man realized that the pope wasn't saying anything at all in response and that he probably didn't have a clue about what he had just spent fifteen minutes or more explaining in relation to his position on the issue. There was an awkward silence. Pope John was the one to speak, thanking the man for his explanation. He then smiled and said, "You must know that I have no idea what you've been saying to me." Then he laughed and pointed to the embarrassed monsignor and said, "Don't worry, you're not alone—Capovilla here tried for nearly two hours last night to explain some of this to me—in depth! I didn't get a lot of what he said, either." But then, turning to the six men, he continued, "I just want all of you to know that the fact that all seven of us can sit at a table together with a sense of truthfulness, integrity, respect, and openness is worthy of my benediction and crucial for us, and so many others. Your presence and attentiveness gives—I hope—all of us hope and begins the process of understanding on many deeper levels." When this incident was reported by various newspapers, some of them said as an aside that some of the representatives were moved to tears, and when they heard his words and the way he presented them, they endeavored to change the way they were speaking and to listen more closely.

The Jewish philosopher Martin Buber spoke and wrote extensively about relationships, communication, and meaning. He is perhaps best known for his book *I and Thou* and the line that became his "signature": "All real living is meeting." The following incident happened in Jerusalem when two students were reading this book and preparing to present their understandings to their class—for their grade. They were engrossed in the text and hit a wall. There was one concept and passage they just didn't understand and couldn't agree on. They argued over interpretations and how they could present it—from the opposing side. They were tired and one of them said, "Enough—hey, isn't Buber in Jerusalem? Let's just ask him to clarify." He was being facetious, but the other student decided to see if they could. He made a phone call, asked for an appointment with Buber, and was surprised that they were put in his schedule within days of the request.

They met with Buber in his office for half an hour. He was the one who began with questions: Could they speak Hebrew? Then, he asked about their backgrounds, families, and where and what they were studying. He then asked them which passage they were having difficulty with (they had shared the reason for their wanting to talk with him with his secretary).

After he read the passage, he asked each of them what they thought it meant. After each one explained what they thought the meaning was, he responded, "Ken, ken"—"Yes! Yes!" which surprised both of them! In Hebrew, to repeat and say a word twice is powerful and it can mean one of two things or both. The first under-standing of the repetition of a word is that it lends emphasis, strength, power to the word; as in the Scripture passage where it reads, "Make justice, justice, your aim." It denotes intensity, passion, and agreement that this is "it," it's essential. The other meaning is that it can refer to the person speaking, implying that both of them under-stood and their interpretations were both true. Buber intended both meanings and complimented them on their work and then gave his interpretation to them—in less than a minute!

Years later, one of the students spoke about his meeting with Buber that day and said that he had no recollection of the passage they had argued over as stu-dents and no memory of what Buber said! He remem-bered nothing of what the room was like or what Buber was wearing or even what the day was like—but he remembered profoundly the sense he had, of himself, of Buber, and the other student as they sat in his presence. He knew the sound of his voice, his tone, his leaning forward to listen, his response to each of them, and that time seemed to pause. Buber's presence wrapped around him. He had made time for them, listened, treated them with dignity, equality, deep interest, and care. The stu-dent always felt like the time was so short, yet in those moments he knew what Buber was talking about: "All real living is meeting"—they were met, embraced, and touched and in the sound of his "Ken, ken," "Yes! Yes!"

He was met, accepted, even cherished. When he told the story, he said that he hoped he shared it in such a way, with such presence and respect, that all who heard it also sensed that they were "met, cherished, and respected." *Yes, Yes* this is listening heart-to-heart.

We shall practice listening so attentively that we are able to hear what the other is saying—and also what is left unsaid. We know that by listening deeply, we already alleviate a great deal of pain and suffering in the other. This powerful listening heart-to-heart can be experienced and practiced in any relationship, but it is sometimes experienced most powerfully when it is in a relationship between a person who is in a position of power or knowledge and one who is seeking help or aid. Anyone in the medical professions, counseling, teaching, or with authority in a religious setting, anyone who has access to what another person needs, is perhaps someone who *needs* to learn to do this kind of listening more than others.

Years ago I copied down this story when I first heard it and then never told it. It was years later that I realized the power in the story and the wisdom it shared about heart-to-heart listening, and I started trying to incorporate it into all my connections with people, especially those in public, after talks, presentations, and even all-day workshops.

Once upon a time, a young woman was apprenticed to a renowned and beloved doctor, also a woman, but growing frail and wanting to share what she had learned with someone who would take her place. The apprentice watched, listened, and read, wanting to treat patients like the doctor did and to care for others like she did—so compassionately. After two years, she started asking the doctor to let her do some of the initial meetings and diagnoses, but the doctor refused. She said, "No, you're not ready yet." But the apprentice was persistent and kept asking, even begging to be allowed to see how she would do when someone came in needing relief and help. Finally, after years of pleading, when she least expected it—they were sitting together on the porch of the clinic resting during the day's heat—a man approached and the doctor turned to her and said— "Here's your chance. You can start with this man."

She leapt up and ran out to meet the man, taking him by the arm and bringing him to the clinic, up the steps and inside. She pulled herself together and reminded herself to act like the doctor, with authority, with her knowledge yet with care and gentleness. Within moments of listening to the man's complaints (they were many) she knew what the man needed: pomegranates. She was instantly relieved—she could do this, she knew what the man was lacking and what would help him. So, she told him firmly that what he needed was to eat pomegranates. He looked at her and kept talking and she spoke firmly again—"Pomegranates, that will help you a lot. Trust me." But the man pushed her away, pulled his arm back, and left, muttering to himself.

She was crushed. What had she done wrong? What else could she have done? She questioned the doctor, who told her that she still hadn't learned much about doctoring, or for that matter, about life or people. She pleaded—"Give me another chance, let me try again." A couple of days later, another patient came up the path to the clinic (another pomegranate patient!). The doctor took her apprentice by the hand, and said—"Stay close, watch, but listen too." The doctor took the woman, elderly but spry, into the clinic, sat her down, gave her a cup of tea, and started asking questions and listened—about her family, garden, husband, and then about her symptoms, her aches and pains. Then she started her examination, interspersing her touch with sounds: "Hmm—ahh—yes... something sweet, but not too sweet, ah, yes, pomegranates, that's it exactly."

The woman responded with a deep sigh and said, "Thank you, thank you, doctor. I just knew you'd know." She went off happy to get her pomegranates! The young apprentice looked at her and said, "I don't understand." The doctor said quietly, "You were correct, your patient needed pomegranates, but more than that, he needed time, and a place to be listened to; he needed your presence." The story reminds us all that what he needed, as all of us do at one time or another, was heart-to-heart listening.

Many people feel that this kind of listening is too hard to do with just anyone or with everyone; they feel that this kind of listening is reserved for friends, loved ones, and occasionally with another in a moment that is often never repeated. But this kind of listening shifts energies within the one listening and, with practice, art, and discipline, can be experienced in listening to and connection with anyone and everyone. It can start with our friends—but perhaps our friends are here to serve as a bridge to changing the way we relate to everyone. The trust we are given by our friends, the confidence, the

ability to risk, dare, and be vulnerable as well as truth-
ful can be shared with many others.

> *In the silence of listening, you can know*
> *yourself in everyone, the unseen singing*
> *softly to itself and to you.*
> —Rachel Naomi Remen[1]

Friendship—what does it mean to be a friend, to
have a friend, to share a friendship? Many mystical traditions, spiritualties, and even the theology of the relationship between God and human beings are described
as friendship. In the Persian Sufi tradition of the thir-
teenth century, Fakhruddin Iraqi defines friendship with
God "as a relationship where God's love precedes the
spiritual traveler's love of God....One can interpret this
to mean that from a Sufi point of view a friend is someone who leads us to experience love and friendliness."[2]
For many people, the experience of friendship, of being
befriended by another, is rare because of its depth, its
intimacy, its endurance through loss, suffering, disagreements; its faithfulness, its truthfulness, and its
sense of being known deeply. It is knowing that the
other is devoted to you in such a way that your needs
are as important to them as their own, if not more so.

In China there is a short story that speaks of friendship in a way that may be new to us. It is told in *Old
History of the Tang Dynasty*:

> Wei Zheng was an extraordinary statesman of
> the early Tang dynasty. He often spoke bluntly

to Emperor Tzizong. After his death, the emperor sighed, "Using bronze as a mirror makes it easy to tidy ourselves up; using history as a mirror makes us clear about the cause of the rise and fall of dynasties; and using other people as a mirror makes us capable of weighing advantages and disadvantages. I often use the three mirrors to examine my faults. Now that Wei Zheng is dead, I have lost one mirror."[3]

The image of the mirror is strong and begins to reveal the power in friendship; it can be shared truth beyond what one would receive from other people. It reveals to us our strengths and our weaknesses, virtues and failures. It is a mirror that also speaks in such a manner that the truth can be heard and taken to heart. This kind of friendship is rare indeed in anyone's life, but this reality is one of the foundations of what a friend is and does for us. When this mirroring becomes mutual, friendship becomes a way of being in communion with another that surpasses and calls forth in us what others might not be able to. Often when this happens, the listening moves into another level, the level of listening soul-to-soul.

Again, there is another Chinese story. I was given it as a gift many years ago. I rarely tell it because it's difficult to tell—to any group on any occasion. It seems to tap into experience in such a way that one hears the story and knows instinctively its truth and it evokes that relationship in everyone in the audience and in the teller. It is simply called "Two Friends."

Once upon a time, there were two friends. One was a gifted lute player, world-renowned, famous, and adored by many. The other just listened to his friend's playing. He listened intently, always amazed at his friend's gift and ability; he enjoyed listening immensely. He attended to each note, each piece, each performance as though each time he heard a piece, it was the first time. This was their relationship, and through the years, the musician would play to his friend and for his friend; even if he couldn't see him in the audience, he was conscious that he was out there, listening. When there were others in the audience who were not receptive or appreciative of his playing, or he was tired and out of sorts, he knew his friend listened and absorbed and shared with him his delight, his presence. Then one day his friend died unexpectedly.

He mourned him, grieving and brokenhearted. He remembered him and what it was like when his friend was with him. For a while he couldn't make music—his sorrow weighed too heavily on him—but then he decided he had to go back to playing, to his schedule, his practices and performances, traveling near and far. He tried, but found out that he couldn't—he didn't have the energy, the strength, the spirit he needed to play—to live as he did before. He felt as though he had lost something of himself—his heart. It took him awhile to realize he felt as though there was no one to listen to him as his friend did—many listened to his music, but his friend had listened to *him*. In sorrow, he cut the strings of his lute. It was the only way he knew to honor his friend.

Years later, he restrung his lute and created a new piece of music in honor of his friend, lost, gone, but within his heart still. He played it in memory of his friend and found that he could play his lute again. It was different of course, but he could, and with time, he was sure that his music was deeper, truer, more resonant, and extended to many others because of his friend's listening. Today in China and in many places in the Far East, it is a ritual to cut the strings of musical instruments when a friend dies.

We know we are blessed when we have a friend like this and hope that we reciprocate that gracefulness, listening, and presence. This is romantic, passionate, and at the extreme of what friendship can be. Another characteristic of friendship is simpler and yet just as comforting and profound. "Two friends are like seashells, they murmur endlessly" (Swahili proverb). Faithfulness, ordinariness, a sense of belonging, even the possibility of communion with each other is part of friendship.

It is said that one of friendship's strongest traits is that the welfare of the other and what the other needs is more important than one's own needs, and it is mutual in this regard. From this experience of being a friend and being befriended, can we learn to listen like this with many others? Once we have experienced this kind of listening—even once—we can have the courage to try and to work hard at listening this way with others. Such an experience of listening within friendship can perhaps be called listening soul-to-soul, listening beyond even heart-to-heart. It might be a rarity, but if we know that experience, we can begin to extend it outward to our other relationships.

FRIENDS OF GOD WHO ARE FRIENDS WITH ALL OTHERS

In the Gospel of John, Jesus tells his followers that they are his friends. God in Jesus is friends with them, with us. He no longer calls us (or treats us as) servants. This is not only a new and intimate way of relating with God, but it is a new way of relating to one another—sharing that friendship we are offered with God, not only by responding to God, but by offering that relationship to all in our lives. This is what Jesus says to his friends:

> As the Father has loved me, so have I loved you. Now remain in my love. If you obey my commands, you will remain in my love, just as I have obeyed my Father's commands and remain in his love. I have told you this so that my joy may be in you and your joy may be complete. My command is this: Love one another as I have loved you. Greater love has no one than this, that he lay down his life for his friends. You are my friends if you do what I command. I no longer call you servants.... Instead I have called you friends, for everything that I learned from my Father I have

made known to you....This is my command: Love each other. (John 15:9–17)

In a sense, that last line could just as easily read, "This is my command: be friends to one another." If we obey, if we listen, if we respond and are open to one another, we remain as friends and we draw others into our friendship with God, and this level of listening, this level of living, is what we can experience as human beings. Being friends with God is definitely listening soul-to-soul, but to extend that into our lives and all our relationships is a good, demanding, and very human and compassionate way to practice one's religion with all others.

The doctor, healer, writer, storyteller, and listener par excellence, Rachel Naomi Remen has said, "Our listening creates a sanctuary for the homeless parts within another person."[4] This kind of listening becomes a way of life, transforming the quality of what it means to be a person. Her books *Kitchen Table Wisdom* and *My Grandfather's Blessings* are filled with stories of her learning to listen and those who taught her this gift. She talks in interviews and articles about recapturing the soul of medicine; "to pursue something stronger than science," namely, to restore a sense of meaning and service through human relationships.[5] In one interview, she speaks of listening, of who we listen to, what stories we listen to, and how that forms us and deforms us. She speaks of the notion of perfection and how destructive it can be.

Dr. Remen: I think perfection is the booby prize in life, actually. It's very isolating, very separating, and it's also impossible to achieve. So you're always struggling to become something you're not. But, you know, this is one of the great—it sounds funny, I was going to say the great joys of working with people on the edge of life. The view from the edge of life is so much clearer than the view that most of us have, that what seems to be important is much more simple and accessible for everybody, which is who you've touched on your way through life, who touched you. What you're leaving behind you in the hearts and minds of other people is far more important than whatever wealth you may have accumulated.

Interviewer Now: What is your understanding of why that simple truth that we've all heard said, and it makes so much sense; why is that hard for us, for human beings to take seriously before we get to that edge of life, or for many of us?

Dr. Remen: I think we get distracted. We get distracted by stories other people have told us about ourselves, that we are not enough, that we will be happy if we have material goods, that material goods will keep us safe. None of these stories are true. What is true is that what we have is each other.[6]

What we have is each other, to listen to each other heart-to-heart, sometimes soul-to-soul, and in that listening and being listened to, we become true. Who we listen to is crucial, for we obey the people we listen to and they can create us, recreate us, redeem us, or separate us from our own truth and the larger truth we are all called to be and become—fully alive human beings. In so much of our life, we are unaware of the power we have with others and how much our listening to them closely can be the difference in what they choose to become.

This last story is one from the Baal Shem Tov, the Master of the Good Name, the founder of eighteenth-century Hassidism (this story was originally in Yiddish). He taught and emphasized that holiness, wholeness, and integrity could be greatly enhanced and learned through storytelling, singing, dancing, and praying in community.

Once upon a time, the Baal Shem Tov was meeting with people, listening to their questions, doubts, troubles, and needs—it seemed he spent most of his days and often part of his nights doing this, and it was exhausting. On this particular day, he was giving gifts to some of his disciples, knowing that when they left on their journeys and returned back to their lives, he may never see them again. He handed out many of his own treasured possessions. Then came one of his dearest disciples, who also happened to be one of the most unassuming, the one who held back, listening, waiting for his teacher, his master, and his friend to speak or invite him to speak. There was nothing left to give. When he came up to him, he was warmly embraced and held tightly, and the Baal Shem Tov whispered in his ear, "To you, I give my stories! You have heard so many of them and taken them to heart. Travel the world and tell my stories. Give them the best gifts I have had to give." The next morning, he left when all the others did, wondering why he was given this gift.

He had always been poor and he was still poor, and he traveled, getting work here and there, telling stories when he could, at night, over meals or drinks in the tavern, but most of the time people weren't interested in his stories. Oh, maybe one or two—but that was more than enough. After years on the road, some of the people he'd come to know told him that they'd heard rumors—stories about a man who was very wealthy and was always interested in stories, and that he paid for every story he was told that he hadn't heard before. He just couldn't get enough of stories. And so Reb Shmuel (his name changes in the various tellings of this story) set out to find this man, so he could improve his fortunes and tell some stories in obedience to his Rebbe's gift. He traveled across great distances and arrived in the Russian city where this man lived, and he sent word to him that he had stories to tell. Immediately, he received an invitation to come to his house, and at a great dinner party, he would be welcomed to tell his stories.

When he arrived, he was surprised to find out that the man was a Jew and that he presided over the community and was a powerful man within the city. It was a beautiful Sabbath meal and as it was ending, the man stood and introduced him, telling his guests that he had been a disciple of the Baal Shem Tov and that the Master had commanded him to tell stories. What an honor this night it would be for them all. So Reb Shmuel stood to tell. He was deeply touched and remembered the Baal Shem Tov's words and warmth as he had been with him that last evening. He opened his mouth...and nothing came out! His mind went utterly blank. He couldn't remember even one story. He was mortified.

The man realized his discomfort and was kind: "Ah, our distinguished guest is weary from his journey. He needs a good night's rest." So he went to bed. The next day at the second meal of Sabbath, he was once again invited to tell a story. To his horror, he went blank again. His host was again kind and explained that he probably needed to eat and pray. They would try again at the last meal of the Sabbath. But it happened again. Sabbath was over and it was time for him to leave, too. Reb Shmeul was ashamed. He had failed the Baal Shem Tov and was bitter that he couldn't even share the one gift he had been given. He was not surprised when his host was cold toward him, and of course, he was not paid anything—he had given nothing. He had already heard what they were calling him now: the man with no stories...and worse.

The sledge set off and the horses were pressed by the host at a fast pace. Then suddenly, Shmuel stood up and yelled, "Stop! Stop! I've got a story. I remember one!" The horses were stopped and standing right where he was, he turned to his host and began, "I hope it's good enough. It's not a long story, in fact it's more something that happened to me." The host nodded. Shmuel spoke, "It was winter and night. The Baal Shem Tov woke me and commanded me to get up, get the horses—we were going out. And I did. We traveled for hours, just the two of us, across the ice and snow, and then we arrived at a mansion, a huge house. Only the Master went in and I waited in the cold, freezing. He was there maybe twenty or thirty minutes and he came out. He got into the sledge and said, 'We're going home.' And we did." Before Shmuel could say anything more, the host began sobbing, crying loudly. Everyone looked at him, amazed and wondering what in that story had affected him so. (A number of the guests at dinner had come with them to drop Shmuel off at a station where he could start his journey home.)

Finally, the host turned and looked at everyone. Slowly he began: "You see, the house and the man the Baal Shem Tov visited that night so long ago was me. I was a very different person then—none of you knew me or who I was or what I did. I had a very high level job in the state, with the Christian church. It was my job to organize forced conversions, with fear tactics and violence against the Jews. When he burst into my house that night, he somehow knew what I was doing and what I was planning. He lamented my soul and how I was destroying so many people, their hopes, their lives, and their beliefs.

"Then he told me that I was Jewish, an orphan who had been given to a couple who kept my origins a secret. I was struck dumb, confounded. Suddenly, what I was doing was terribly wrong and worse now that I knew I was doing it to my own people. I broke down and told him I would change and become a Jew—what I truly was. But, I asked him, 'How will I ever know that I've been forgiven, that I have tried to undo all the harm that I have done?' The Baal Shem Tov told me that night, 'When the night comes when someone tells you this story, that is when you know you are forgiven, and you are becoming who you truly are meant to be!' I have longed in silence for this story to come to me, for someone to set me free. I have waited so long to hear this story; to listen to a story and know it's mine, and tonight my heart rejoices, my heart's prayer and hope has been heard, and as I listened to this story, my story told, I know my life is beginning yet again and who knows, what I shall become." *Listen Here!*

All listening begins in silence. Now we will go into silence to listen and to seek the source and depths of all sound, stillness, and potent emptiness. Rearrange the letters of *listen* and you discover what is *silent*. This task of being good listeners, heart-to-heart, soul-to-soul, begins as one of the sages wrote: in silence and in waiting, in inwardness, in each of our own souls.

REFLECTIONS AND PRACTICES

1. As you read the stories of friendship here, did you remember your own stories? Do you have a friend who listens to you as the man listened to his friend's music and to his soul? Do you listen to another person this way?

2. To listen heart-to-heart and soul-to-soul can radically alter what you think you know or believe, even shatter your own surety when it comes to the truth, the bedrock that you stand on. Read this quote:

   In life, you don't get all the answers at once.
   First you must absorb and live with one
   simple truth. Then, later, you must find

another truth—one that may seem to conflict with and negate all you previously learned.

Then from that confusion, emerges a higher truth—the inner light behind all you had learned before.[7]

This experience often follows listening heart-to-heart or soul-to-soul to another person. Have you ever experienced this in your life? What was it like, and how did you live with it afterward?

3. Try to go visit someone you know who is elderly, or ill, or homebound. Or chose someone you want to get to know. Then go sit and try to listen to them heart-to-heart, as a friend of God with them, drawing them out, asking them questions, attentive to everything about them. After, reflect on what you learned—about them, about yourself, and about listening.

5

SILENCE

The small truth has words that are clear;
the great truth has great silence.
                              —Rabindranath Tagore

Paradoxically, this chapter will be a whole segment filled with words, quotes, stories, images, and descriptions of silence and listening to silence, and beyond silence. There are so many kinds of silence: the stillness just before the crack of dawn; the outer reaches of the universe and space; the silence of the stars; the heavy silence of noon-day heat; and heavier still, the silence when one has heard the hard truth about oneself; the eerie quiet after the clap of thunder, waiting for the lightning flash to follow; the exhausted silence after the whine of missiles and the sound of bombs; the devastating terror of silence in that moment of stepping on a land mine, knowing your next movement will be your last; the silence of resignation, of the sudden realization that pain has stopped.

The silence of certain places: an empty old chapel, cave, church carrying silences of time and burdens left

94

behind; the silence of thin air at the top of mountains or other extremes geographically, in the sere desert, and in moments when all the background noises cease in the jungle.

The silence of a long hush of people praying without words together when one can feel as though they have stumbled into a moment of shared intimacy. The empty silence of grief and mourning that seems to carve out a space inside us that goes beyond emptiness. The silence of expectation, waiting, hoping, fearing for a diagnosis, news of a dear one's safety, the birth of a child, and another's death. There is the silent screaming that is a form of prayer in the Jewish community, and it is the abiding silence of peace, a sense of wholeness and holiness that is a rare gift in the presence of some people, a sense of belonging, of being alive—but it is always a gift.

Silence—what is it? Where does it come from? What is its source? A certain man who went into the woods to find himself and to listen there to what was all around him and what was within him said, "Silence is the universal refuge, the sequel to all dull discourses and all foolish acts, a balm to our every chagrin, as welcome after satiety as after disappointment."

Henry David Thoreau, this man who spent time in a small cabin on the edge of his town, wrote in his journal about another kind of silence that he had become aware of as well: "Silence is the communing of a conscious soul with itself. If the soul attends for a moment to its own infinity, then and there is silence. She is audible to all men, at all times, in all places, and if we will we may always harken to her admonitions."[1] It is this other kind of silence, binding what is out there with what is within, that Christopher Jamison, OSB, described so succinctly when he wrote about the people who went on an eight-day silent retreat at a monastery. After just forty-eight hours, they all started to discover and see that "silence is a path to hidden dimensions of life."[2]

So it appears that there is silence without or outside the human person, silence within the human body—in the mind, heart, and soul—and silence beyond sound, beyond all these silences. This quiet, this stillness we covet as human beings, is one of our innate needs for survival. The poet W. B. Yeats tried to express it this way: "We can make our minds so like still water that beings gather about us so that they may see their own images, and so to live for a moment with a clearer, perhaps even with a fiercer life, because of our quiet."[3] Whatever this stillness, this silence is—it is dynamic, full of energy and power and can draw others into communion as well as center and concentrate our own sensibilities. Again, Yeats attested to its importance: "The journey into the inner self is not just the important one, it is the only one. We need to listen to the sound beyond the silence."

There is a story from the native peoples of the Northwest coast of the United States and Canada simply called "The Heron" that captures a bit of this essence that we call quiet, or stillness or silence. The character of Raven in the story can be just a raven—they are everywhere, or Raven can be a trickster who steals from everyone. In this image, Raven is a wise one, a sage, a seer who shares wisdom with the people, and sometimes Raven is the Great Spirit.

Once upon a time, it was late autumn. The cold was coming, the air had already shifted one morning and the summer softness was gone. Everyone had their tasks to do and so much had to be done for everyone to be ready for winter. There was food to cache, wood to stack, clothes to be mended; even the children were kept busy with their small tasks. It was still early evening and eagles soared over the waters, the salmon were swimming, even the otters were playing on the beach, but no one stopped to admire them and to appreciate the fullness of life all around them.

Raven was watching the people and noticed two old ones, a man and woman, husband and wife. They were sitting still on a log. Raven (who is female in this story) knew what the couple sitting side by side were thinking. The man was imagining the next morning when he would rise early, steal away to the other side of the bay to his favorite spot, and stand silently fishing. He would become as still as the early morning waters. The woman was imagining that she would rise early, and once her husband had left, she would wrap herself in her warm blanket and go out to walk along the shore. She would see what the tide washed up, collect a few shells or other treasures, and she too would stand silent at the water's edge watching the sun come to bless the land and the people for another day. Raven was pleased and went to perch on the log beside them.

Raven spoke with them: "Ah, you are wise ones. You have found the balance and know when to be busy and when to stop, just sit, just be, and swallow the quiet. There are many things to do, but the stillness must be honored, and we must drink it in so that our souls and bodies are in harmony and we all take the time to honor the Great Spirit's creations."

Raven decided to give the two old ones a gift. "You both love the heron that you watch in the morning that stands so still in the waters, waiting, that it is hard to separate the heron out from the waters and the sky. I'm going to give you the knowledge and the power to turn people into herons! They can breathe deeply and call back their souls from where they have roamed in the night. They can know what it's like to be so still as to be invisible to many; to see clearly, thankful for their place on the earth; to listen to the silence and breathe it in deeply; to quiet their thoughts and hold their life in their hands in peace. It is best done early, before dawn and then as the sun comes up, stronger with each moment, they will return again to their human form, but they will carry with them all that they have learned and experienced so that they might live their day in deeper communion with all the people."

So, they say, each morning before the light opens the eyes of the day, anyone can stand still, look for the heron, be at peace with all around them, and know when to be quiet and when to work and how to make sure that the important things are attended to—caring for the poor, the weak, and those who are strangers, and working with all the Great Spirit has made together.

[Snap your fingers!] Now, you are all herons! Be still and practice. It doesn't last long and soon you will be shifting back into your human forms. Be still!

This is a story that draws us into quiet and stills us

and pushes all other thoughts to the edges of our minds. It lets us become aware of the silence all around us. It captures a momentary sense of what silence is and the effects it can have on us that linger beyond the time of stillness.

In "A Thing of Silence" (included in the collection *Ethics of the Fathers*) Rabban Gamliel's son, Rabbi Shimon, writes, "All my life I have been raised among the wise, and I have found nothing better for the body than silence." In turn, Rabbi Yanki Tauber comments on this passage, saying, "Alone in a verbose world, the soul of man [woman] is a thing of silence. Its mission in life is to impart silence to the world about it."[4]

> *When peaceful silence lay over all,*
> *and night had half run her swift course,*
> *your all-powerful Word leapt down*
> *from Heaven.*
>
> —Wisdom 18:14–15

All the traditions of the world speak of the Silence that is beyond quiet, beyond stillness, beyond sound, that brushes us outwardly in our senses and bodies but can be known or experienced within our persons, in our minds, hearts, and souls, and yet is the Unknown beyond all things. Trying to talk about this mystery within all things, outside of all things, and beyond all things is harder to speak about than the experience of simple silence and quiet that is physical or earthly and sensate. People in all times of history from all over the world have spoken of it and sought to share its power and its essence with others. This piece is from the tradition of the Quakers, the Religious Society of Friends, whose worship practice is steeped in sitting in silence as a community, allowing what they call the "Light Within" to emerge and grow stronger within each of them, and as a body together:

> Deep within us all is an amazing inner sanctuary of the soul, a holy place, a Divine Center, a Speaking Voice to which we may continuously return. Eternity is at our hearts pressing upon our time-torn lives, warming us with intimations of an astounding destiny, calling us home unto Itself. Yielding to these persuasions, gladly committing ourselves in body and soul, utterly and completely, to the Light Within, is the beginning of true light.[5]

This awareness of this hidden though easily found and entered into place or part of our very being as humans has been discovered by many—those gathering for worship and prayer alone and with others and those solitary persons as they face hardship, isolation, imprisonment, and violent death at the hands of other human beings. Etty Hillesum, a young Jewish woman, struggled to live deeply and with hope, with freedom and passion, and with meaning as she watched Hitler begin to move on her people, seeking to exterminate them. As long as she could, she went about her daily life, studying, writing, making music, being involved with her friends and lover, and then as the noose was pulled tighter about her, she knew she would not escape the fate of her people and was put on a train bound for the camps, where she died. She wrote this in her journal close to the time she was going to die: "There is a really deep well inside me. And in it dwells God...but more often stones and grit block the well, and God is buried beneath. Then God must be dug out again."[6] Her words are strong, sure, and wrenching, and the truth of them, known and experienced, even relied on somehow, leaps off the page into that really "deep well inside" us, too.

The Sufi mystic Jalaluddin Rumi wrote in his voluminous collection of poetry, "Why are you so afraid of silence? Silence is the root of everything. If you spiral into its void, a hundred voices will thunder messages you long to hear. Silence is the language of God; all else is poor translation." This silence isn't heard. This silence though, can be sensed, can be listened to, can be absorbed. This silence can listen to us and absorb us.

For many, this silence is intimately bound to the Great Mystery, the Holy, the Great Spirit, the Shekhinah, the Holy Presence, any name for God, and yet is known as Emptiness, Nothingness, Nada. The Dominican preacher of the 13th century in Europe, Meister Eckhart, stated it simply: "Nothing resembles the language of God so much as does silence." The monk, Thomas Merton referred to it as "the hidden wholeness at the heart of things." Getting to this hidden wholeness, this heart of things, the place of stillness is work, is a discipline, and a choice to return to again and again.

Many people start in a place, a space that is away from sound, a place apart, but then there are still the sounds in our own minds that are harder to get past. In Zen, this is sometimes called "monkey mind," jumping all over the place. As someone who has spent a good deal of time in Ireland, Scotland, and New Zealand, I call it "the sheep are loose," my mind straying in every direction, wandering off; others call it "herding the cats." We are constantly distracted by our own thoughts, talking to ourselves, and what is swirling around inside us. Someone once said that God is constantly whispering truth to us in our ears and in our deepest, inmost places—in the Silence—but we're too busy talking, even what we call praying, and we don't listen. One weekly reflection from The Institute for Contemplative Practice says,

> Sound and silence are not necessarily opposites. There is a sound in silence that is non-audible. Many people find it easier to meditate or pray in a silent place, because by blocking out the audible sounds that pull our attention outward, we can bring our attention inward and focus on hearing our inner silence which is our True Self.
>
> In Islamic spirituality, this inaudible sound is referred to as "Hu," the basic vibration in the universe. "Hu" is also a Holy Name of God. When we seek to immerse ourselves in Silence, we are not trying to block out the sounds we hear, but rather increase our ability to hear the very specific sound of our True Self.[7]

This silence is both vast and as tiny as a mustard seed, and it is alive, pulsing, capable of stilling us, and at the same time transforming and changing us.

The first time I witnessed the amazing, shocking, and gorgeous display of the Northern Lights, the Aurora Borealis, in the frigid winter night skies, they shimmered constantly in motion and yet were motionless, continually changing and yet stationary, every hue and color, and it was so quiet. The silence was almost tangible, enveloping. It was sound without sound, and it drew you in—and down—and rooted you deeper into the ground while bent backward and pulled up to the dance of the sky.

This phenomenon in the natural world tries to speak of this silence within us individually and universally that is somehow a path into the center of all life, all matter and spirit. Many people are reluctant to call it God or think of it and relate to it as a deity, instead seeking to see it as a grounding, a centering, a balancing of their own energies, their body, mind, and spirit, in harmony with all others and with creation. Many people believe and have known it as both realities. But in any case, this is the way one woman, Mother Maribel of Wantage, describes it: "Silence is not a thing we make; it is something into which we enter. It is always there."

Edith Stein, a Jewish woman philosopher who became a cloistered Carmelite nun and was arrested and executed in a Nazi concentration camp, spoke of this interior silence. She used metaphors of the natural world and shifted into the realm of the Spirit. When she describes the power, the movement, and the sound—"the torrent that is the Spirit of God"—in the soul, one has the sense that she is speaking from her own experience.

> Just as the torrent that bursts its banks sub-
> merges everything beneath its waters, fills all
> the deep places and drowns out every other
> noise with the roar of its waves, so the soul, in
> the same way, is empowered by "this torrent
> that is the spirit of God. He takes hold of her
> with such power that she feels as if all the
> rivers of the world were flooding in on her."
> Yet, the vehemence of this flood does not cause
> her any pain, for they are rivers of peace, and
> their onslaught "fills her completely with peace
> and glory." The water fills the depths of lowli-
> ness and the void of her desires, and in the
> whirlpool of the current, she hears "a spiritual
> voice that...is louder than every other voice and
> is heard over all the noises of the world."[8]

This is her personal being known in this silence that is thunderous. Even the language she uses to describe what it is like is contradictory and filled with opposites. It is "this" and it is "that" and it is "not this" and "not that." And then she connects her own experience to what she believes is also a communal experience, to the coming of the Spirit of the risen Lord upon his friends and followers at the festival called Pentecost:

> It is a great thundering interior voice that fills
> the soul with strength and power, just as it did
> when it accompanied the descent of the Holy

Spirit on the Apostles. The mighty wind that the inhabitants of Jerusalem heard was only a sign of what the Apostles perceived interiorly. Despite its formidable power, this spiritual voice is gentle to the ear. St. John perceived it as "the roaring of mighty waters and the rolling sounds of thunder," and, at the same time, as "a concert of harpists playing their harps."[9]

Jesus himself describes this inner silence as living waters within the one who believes that can be a continuous source of life for them and for all others. "Jesus stood up and said in a loud voice: 'If anyone is thirsty, let them come to me and drink. Whoever believes in me, as the Scripture has said, streams of living water will flow from within them.' By this he meant the Spirit, whom those who believe were later to receive. Up to that time the Spirit had not been given, since Jesus had not yet been glorified" (John 7:37–39).

For Christians, this silence is the presence of the Spirit of the risen Lord and the Father who spoke to him as Word made flesh; this silence is the Trinity. To seek this silence is to yearn for the life of God more deeply and truly. It is a given. It is there, here, within us and all people, and in all creation.

This is a powerful Silence for the Jewish people as well. It is the ever-present revelation of God. Rabbi Rami Shapiro told this story:

This silence was "catching" for all around him seated at the table, while "many others passed hours in heated Torah discussion, punctuated by much music and dancing. But at the table of Reb Menachem Mendel of Vorki, very little was said, for the rebbe's way was the way of silence. Hours passed and not a word was spoken. Even the breathing of those assembled fell into silence, and only the buzzing of an occasional fly broke the silence." When the meal was finished and they left for their homes, some of the reb's followers approached a visiting Reb and asked him how he found the quality of their rabbi's "tish" (a meal shared by a rabbi and his followers and friends with commentary and teaching on the Torah portion). This was his reply! "What a tish the rebbe gave! He taught me lessons in Torah I have heard nowhere else! Every one of his challenges tore down my understanding of Torah and rebuilt it from the ground up. But I didn't take his challenge passively. I answered every question he asked of me!" The followers of Reb Menachem sighed, relieved—they knew the visitor understood, heard the Silence and was one of them. (oral tradition)

In the commentary that is attached to this story, this is what is written:

Revelation is immediate and momentary, continuous rather than continual. It comes through intuition rather than logic; it is right-brained rather than left. To hear it, you must be silent. But being silent is not the same as being passive. You have to offer all you know to the silence and allow it to be torn down. What is torn down is what you know; what is built up is what you don't know. But the new becomes the old, and so the sacrifice must be made again and again.

Rest on nothing, and your foundation is secure.[10]

This story and comment reveals one of the difficulties of stopping and sinking into silence. What we hear may disturb us and not be what we want to hear. What we experience may shake us thoroughly to our core. We may be afraid of what we find in the silence. All of us at one time or another are afraid of being alone—from experiencing what it is to be in solitude and alone, to experiencing loneliness and what isolates, separates us from others and reality and can become depression, even despair. Entering our deepest, truest reality and the reality of the Silence, the deepest Truth and Presence, which is vast, other, and demanding, can be terrifying as well as consoling, enlightening, engaging, and transformative. We often look for distractions intentionally, anything that will keep us from having to face that Silence and know that we might need to change, radically, even continually, in order to be authentic and true to our own reality of who we are as human beings. This kind of silence can lead us face-to-face with our lacks, our failures, our dishonesty, our lack of integrity, falseness, and what we do to avoid anything that is painful about our past, our present, and in the people and the world around us. So we run and hide from any silence, let alone The Great Silence that is always holding us, albeit unawares.

We want to know the truth about ourselves, but at the same time, we are afraid of it or afraid of seeing the great gap and disparity between who we are and who we pretend to be. Silence brings out an approach/avoidance pull in us that is strong and almost instinctive until we can know that Silence as healing, comforting, and trans-figuring as well as confrontational, demanding change, and painfully honest. Dr. Howard Thurman (1899–1981), a great preacher in the African American community, grew up in Florida during segregation and constantly struggled against the denigrating and violent experience that he faced as a young black man in the South. In this dehumanizing environment, he sought to uncover a sense of who he might be other than what society was telling him. In a recent article on Thurman in *Hospitality*, the newspaper of The Open Door Community—Hospitality and Resistance in the Catholic Worker Movement, based in Atlanta—Catherine Meeks writes about what sourced him in his own quest for self-identity.

> His faith helped him with his quest. There was also the teaching of his grandmother, a woman of great spiritual strength and faith. The gifts from her, and his keen mind and open heart, led him to seek God in the silence of the dark nights, in thunderstorms and in all the places

where only the listening heart can hear the still, small voice of God.

She quotes him on what is genuine in every person from a sermon he preached at Spelman College in Atlanta. It was at a baccalaureate for young women leaving to begin their adult lives in a tumultuous time and a time that would call for them to decide what was the deepest truth of their lives.

There is in every person something that waits for the sound of the genuine in herself. There is in you something that waits and listens for the sound of the genuine in yourself. Nobody like you has ever been born and no one like you will ever be born again—you are the only one. And if you miss the sound of the genuine in you, you will be a cripple all the rest of your life, because you will never be able to get a scent on who you are.

This genuineness that is seeded in us can only be developed, nurtured, and matured in seeking this silence that is a seed covering that protects our inner truth, our core, our soul from any culture, reality, or experience that can destroy us, or make us less than who we are born to be. In silence, we seek and find a profound acknowledgment of this genuineness that connects us to our deepest selves and to others. It sustains life and creates us anew. We need silence as much as we need water, food, shelter, and companionship to become and be human.

THE WAYS INTO SILENCE

Forms of meditation, sitting, walking, doing simple tasks repeatedly, as in raking the sand around stones in Zen temple gardens, peeling piles of potatoes in preparation for meals, washing dishes—any common task—can serve as the "way into silence" that is within and around us, yet beyond us and other than our silences. Many teaching stories of Zen, parables of Jesus and Jewish sages, Native American tales told only at proscribed times of the seasons, all seek to quantum leap us into this Silence or trip us up so that we fall into this Silence that is sometimes called enlightenment, awareness, consciousness, heightened presence, mystical experience, being known by the Unknown Unknowable —the litany is endless as we seek to speak of what this Silence might be.

All of this discourse on Silence and our way through silence into this Silence beyond silence can be extremely serious and heavy. I once saw a bumper sticker that nearly made me drive off the road I laughed so hard. It read, "Ask me about my vow of silence!" Sometimes one can be thrown into silence—the trick is to then settle in for a longer duration and listen with one's heart and soul, even though it wasn't planned at that moment or place.

Years ago when I spent some time in a monastery outside Tokyo, the master told a story about a mouse that is "stuck" inside each of us:

Once upon a time, there was a mouse, like all the other mice. She scurried around, looking for food to eat, and to store away. She was always on the lookout for the monastery cat and she even avoided most humans—they didn't often react kindly or quietly to her presence when sighted. She was busy with mice things. But every once in a while, this mouse would stop and just stand there—even out in the open where it was dangerous. She would freeze, lift her head, cock it to one side as though she was hearing something, listening hard. She'd squint and narrow her eyes even more than mice can do, and her whiskers would wiggle and her whole body would tremble. She would turn to the other mice and say, "Do you hear a roaring in your ears? Isn't it strange? Isn't it wonderful? If only I could find it. I know it's meant for me, for all mice. This roaring in our ears, it keeps beckoning, inviting."

When I first heard this story, it was just strange and weird and indecipherable, but then, many of the koans and teaching stories were! And I was not alone in my confusion. But in the years since—that roaring is apt. Even the sense of smallness, yet connectedness, of relationship and the invitation beyond the business of being a mouse—it all speaks volumes of this Silence.

When I told this story once in Thailand, I was shocked to hear one of the monks there respond with: "Of course! It's the roaring of the resurrection! I never expected that!" And yet, what a theological conversation that started in the group, followed by a half hour of mediation that drew us all down deeper into the silence within ourselves that we shared as a rare gift—together.

Then, in the last year or two, I read this reflection by Enzo Bianchi, the founder of the ecumenical monastic Bose Community in Italy (begun in 1965 and still strong today). It began to draw together what an individual's silence was, the silence of Jesus, the Silence that holds the universe together and the Silence that is beyond what words might be—an edge to awareness or knowing.

> In Christianity we contemplate Jesus Christ as the Word made flesh, but also as the silence of God. The gospels show us a Jesus who, as he goes towards the Passion, increasingly refrains from speaking and enters into silence, like a mute lamb. One who knows the truth and the inexpressible ground of reality neither wants nor is able to betray the ineffable in speech but protects it with his silence. Jesus, "who does not open his mouth" (Isaiah 53.7), reveals that silence is what is truly strong. He makes his silence an action, and by doing so he is able to make his death an act, the gesture of a living person. In this context it should be clear that behind both words and silence, what truly saves is the love that gives life to both. Who is the crucified Christ if not the icon of silence, the silence of God himself?[11]

Listening, in all its varied forms and levels, is a fundamental attitude of life and a source for life itself. Listening interiorizes what is drawn in from the ear to the heart, and yet our own inner space is at its source silent. Our interior stillness must be resourced, visited, and touched regularly so that it can ground us, concentrate us, and draw us back to the truth of who we are before The Silence. Silence generates compassion, freedom, awareness, humility (a sense of being close to the earth, in right relation to all else in the world and others), truthfulness, justice and love. But we have to come to recognize our need for silence—on all levels. Dietrich Bonhoeffer wrote, "Inherent in silence is a marvelous power of observation, clarification, and concentration on the things that are essential."[12]

In this same chapter 29, "Silence," Bianchi quotes Girolamo Savonarola: "The father of prayer is silence, the mother of prayer is solitude." He continues:

> Silence alone makes listening possible—in other words, it alone allows us to welcome within us not only the Word but also the presence of the One who speaks. Through silence we awaken to the experience of the indwelling God, because the God we seek by following the risen Christ in faith is a God who is not outside of us, but who dwells within us. In the fourth Gospel Jesus says, "Those who love me will keep my word, and my Father will love them, and we will come to them and make our home with them." (John 14:23). Silence is a language of love, of depth, of being present to another. It is the experience of love, it is a language that is often much more eloquent, intense and communicative than a word.[13]

I quote this paragraph because it specifically mentions the deep and abiding connection among silence, solitude, and prayer in the Christian tradition. I have not spoken of prayer or of contemplation—the prayer that is silent, wordless in silence, with The Silence encompassing all that is created, uniting us in compassion and communion, sourcing our lives in the Trinity. That is another book! This segment on Silence is just a primer—a basic introduction to silence in listening and listening to silence—externally in the world around us, internally within us in layers and levels, and to the Silence that encompasses all sound and is beyond sound, and other than sound; that is one way of encountering God. Daring to be still, to sit in silence, to pursue silence in time and space alone and with others; to be drawn to silence, by Silence is genesis—a beginning, our beginnings. In silence, from silence, everything shifts and all things, especially words and understanding, articulate meaning differently and give us ears, hearts, and souls to listen more closely, more truly, and more in communion with all.

To draw this section to a close, there is an old and ever new story. It has a number of names, but the name I give it is "Silence to Silence."

Once upon a time, there was a very wise and holy rabbi. Besides his many duties as rabbi and leader of his community, he was a teacher, a counselor, an "ear" for anyone who would come for his insights, advice, and just to talk—he would listen. One day a couple came to speak with him because they were very concerned about their young son who was unruly, undisciplined—never wanting to be still, study the Torah, learn his lessons, even go to bed! (He was afraid that he would miss out on something.) They just didn't know what to do. What did he suggest? The rabbi sat still and quiet for a moment and then said, "Bring your son to me and we will have a talk together." They breathed a sigh of relief—of course, the rabbi could do what they couldn't, and because he was such a strong figure and personality, their son would listen to him!

The very next day, the young boy, who was around six years old, was brought into the rabbi's study. To their surprise, the rabbi asked his parents to leave the child with him for about a half hour. Then they could come back and collect him. They left and the young boy watched them go with a bit of terror on his face. They had told him why they were bringing him to the rabbi—of all things! He only knew the rabbi from a distance, in the synagogue. He towered over the boy and his voice filled the whole synagogue, when he spoke and sung and prayed. The boy stood on the other side of the rabbi's large desk and was slowly backing toward the door.

The rabbi pushed his chair back from the desk and motioned the boy to come around to his side of the desk. Hesitantly, fearfully, almost in tears, the boy obeyed. There was a large window behind them looking out into the woods, and the rabbi lifted the boy onto his lap and turned to look out the window into the quiet of the trees and afternoon light. He didn't say a word. He held the boy close to his heart and the boy's own heart was racing, pounding madly. He held him in the silence. Soon the boy stilled and quieted and leaned against the old man's heart, listening to its rhythm and beating. They sat together for the whole half hour. Then the rabbi said,

"I think your parents will be here soon." The boy looked up at him and smiled and climbed down. Then the rabbi said, "Whenever you want to come and visit, you just tell my wife that you need to see me." The boy nodded. And the knock came on the door.

The parents came in to find their son standing near the rabbi who was standing too. They didn't know what to say, but the rabbi assured them that he'd had a heart-to-heart talk with the boy and there would be no problems in the future. "If he ever wants to come back, that's good—there will always be time for him." He blessed them and they turned to leave, but the young boy turned at the door, smiled, waved at the rabbi, and bowed just a little bit into the silence.

REFLECTIONS AND PRACTICES

1. Reflect on your own routine of making space for silence in your life. If you don't have one, begin. Start slowly, with ten or fiteen minutes at most, twice a day. It can be in the morning and evening, or at times in your day that you know you can have to yourself, apart and alone. (It's interesting to note that many classical music stations have a segment in the early afternoons around 1 or 2 p.m. that they describe as "time alone in the midst of your work day" that lasts just about ten to fifteen minutes. It is time to stop, to unwind, and to just be—and listen! Do this with silence.)

2. Pick your time to be silent and your place. Then begin. Perhaps this bit from John Dear's journal while he was staying as a visitor at Thomas Merton's hermitage might help to get you started.

> I have a Zen koan for you to ponder, he says turning to me. ["What is the sound of listening?"] He pauses and looks at me intently. The fire crackles. The sound of listening?
>
> We are born into listening, he observes, and we die into listening. Spend every minute here at the hermitage, like Merton, listening for the Spirit, letting the Spirit breathe in you and come alive in you. That's what prayer is all about. You need no books, nothing at all. Just sit. Breathe in. Breathe out. And listen. It's that simple.[14]

3. *Listen Here!* Practice doesn't necessarily make perfect, but it makes the open door more apparent and walking through it easier, appreciating its thousands of forms and places.

6

MUSIC AND NOISE

*Music is pleasing not only because of the
sound but because of the silence that is in it:
without the alteration of sound and silence
there would be no rhythm.*
    —Thomas Merton, *No Man Is an Island*

We will come from silence, begin with music, and
progress to noise, make our way back through music,
and end in silence once again. We will begin with sound
that is music with an ancient story from Korea, probably from the Silla Dynasty (57 BC–AD 935). It was one
of the most powerful, wealthy, artistic, and autocratic
periods in Korean history. Koreans, as with many other
Asian peoples, honor filial piety and devotion, honoring
the ancestors and their wisdom and obeying the traditional customs handed down to them. All of these are
the foundation of this story.

Once upon a time, long ago when King Heungduk-
wang, was the forty-second king of Silla, there lived an
old woman. She was growing feeble, her long hair the

color of the moon, tied in a bun. She lived with her son and daughter-in-law, whose heart was as fine and lovely as a strip of rare brocade, and young grandson who was the delight of all their lives; she was always treated with great respect. She was kept warm in winter, with the heaviest blanket and jacket. In the days when it was hot, her bed was put near the window to get a cross breeze. She was seated first when it was time to eat and given the choicest portions of the fish or meat and served first with the rice. Her son would travel far to the coast to get the fish that she loved, and her daughter-in-law would cook it just the way she liked it. Of course, she was given the best and largest portion, but she doted on her grandson who would sit beside her and she would feed him tiny pieces off her plate. In fact, she did this at every meal—making sure the child ended up with the best and the largest portion.

At every meal, her son and his wife watched them and worried, and they would talk about it at night, softly keeping their voices down so that she could not hear them. They were concerned about her health and concerned that she was not getting enough food—they had to be so careful about sharing the food, as they were very poor. They tried to take the child out to play at meal times or let him continue playing while they ate— but to no avail. She would wrap up pieces to keep for the boy and make sure he got them later. Their child was growing strong and was very healthy, but she was growing feebler by the day.

One night while they were talking, he told his wife, "I am worried, distressed about what is happening. What are we to do? You know the saying: 'We may always have another child but I will never have another mother.'" His wife heard the words and her heart wrenched and ached, and she knew that her husband had been thinking of this for a long time and had come to a terrible decision. He continued saying, "I'm afraid it must be done. Tomorrow we must take our son and remove him from us so that my mother may live long." His wife was broken-hearted and she struggled against the teachings she had known since she was little, that she must obey her husband and help him destroy their child and her overwhelming love for her baby. She did not sleep. Her husband didn't either.

But the next morning, they both climbed a hill near their house. She carried the child and he carried a shovel. They found a good place, with a view of their house and a far horizon and he began to dig. She wept silently so as not to wake the child. He dug down deeper, and suddenly there was a sound! He hit something hard that sent out a sound—it sang out! He dug more quickly and found a bell! It was a simple bell, but well crafted, made of stone and heavy. He rang it softly, then harder, and the sound rang out on the air, fine and pure.

The woman turned to her husband in joy and grabbed his arm. This must be a sign from our ancestors. They have given us a bell, a gift telling us that our son must live. Let us keep the bell, fill in the hole, go home, and see what the bell is announcing with its sound, what it is telling us that is coming. The husband was as eager as she was to find a reason not to kill his child. They went down with the child and the bell and hung it outside their front door, on their small porch.

They went on living but now listening to the bell whenever the wind touched it softly or stronger as the wind rose before a storm. When someone rang the bell, it had another sound—as though each person ringing it shared their song with the stone bell. In time, everyone began to speak of the bell. Many decided that its sound must be a result of its being so old and made differently than the bells you could get nowadays. Some people said it reminded them of the joyous sound of the geese returning in spring. Others said it sounded like cold clear mountain water running over stones. Each person seemed to hear something that gladdened them and stirred their hearts—in fact people started coming to visit the family just to hear what sound the bell would make. They were hungry for its sound but the sound lingered inside them, and many people found themselves smiling as though they knew a secret long after the echo of the bell receded on the air.

Time passed and one day, they say, the sound of the bell rung by the strong wind carried farther than before—all the way to the king's palace. The king thought he heard dragonfly wings moving near his ear, light and soft and calming. He wanted whatever produced that haunting sound. He summoned his servant and told him to find it. Within days, a servant returned to the king, telling him of the bell and the husband and wife, their child and the old woman and the story. To the dismay of the family, they also brought back the bell to the king. The king was proud of the man and his wife who sought to obey the old ways and how they cared for their aged mother. It was the servant who also told the king of their poverty and their desperation, moving the king to give the family land so that they would not go hungry again. But they wanted their bell back and petitioned the king and asked too that their neighbors be given land as well, for they were all poor and hungry and caught in the vise of what they should do with their children and their elderly relatives. To everyone's surprise and delight, the king agreed and sent the bell back and renamed the village Chong-dong—the village of the bell. He told them to remember that devoted hearts can move even heaven itself! The people said that the sound of the bell had moved even the king to think of others beside himself and his wealth, but they didn't let him hear that thought.

They say the family lived well; there were sons and daughters to play with the first child, and the mother-in-law lived long; even their neighbors prospered. But that was long ago and no one remembers where the village was—and so the bell has been lost. Now all that remains is the sound of the story for you to hold and share—and the sound of the bell that now sings in your souls. This is the shared wisdom that each sound echoes in us reminding us of our own sound, our own song that sings our soul.

The story is one of hope, of hanging on for a dearer life, and it stirs inside of us the sense that, at root, life is good, holy, whole and that we are capable of incredible, amazing, creative, and life-giving responses to anything that can happen. In the same way, this is often exactly what music does for us—expressing the inexpressible but deeply felt and known wisdom of resources within us and our traditions and histories. Perhaps the difference between music and what we call "noise" is the ability or inability to hear and listen to the music that dwells innately in everything. One person's music, literally, can be another person's grating noise and dissonance.

In our lives, there are layers of sound: our heating and air conditioning systems, innumerable media devices whether in public buildings, elevators, planes, never-ending ring tones of our or others' phones, timers from microwaves, coffee pots, alarms, or more personally coming into our ears through earphones or bleeding out of others' iPods, and so on. There is street noise, traffic, sonic booms, airplanes, factories, subways, rail systems, radios, public address systems—a seemingly endless interruption or background din, hum, drone, and rude interruptions. The level of loudness can be overwhelming whether we are aware of it or not—affecting our immune systems, heart rate, blood pressure, and even what we eat/drink and how much and how fast we consume it. It is said that in very loud environments, we eat less but drink more. There is the inevitable hearing loss, but decibel levels at certain frequencies affect our cardiovascular systems—and hours later, the effects are still measureable. Along with noise, we tend to associate clutter, stress, demands, agendas, and what needs to be done, with loudness—as though physical and psychological realities become attached to sounds that we lump into negative categories.

Of course, this noise is most noticeable in cities worldwide, from Delhi to New York, from Dublin to Singapore, but it's in every small town and neighborhood.

Manmade sounds fill the air. Discordant demands intrude upon our minds, and in response, we often start speaking and acting louder ourselves, raising our voices, becoming aggressive and demanding of others and our surroundings. The reports say,

> Among environmental factors in Europe, environmental noise leads to a disease burden that is second in magnitude only to that from air pollution, says a 2011 World Health Organization report. In the United States, noise is now the number one neighborhood complaint, beating out crime and traffic, according to the American Housing Survey conducted by the US Census. There have been incidents of noise conflicts leading to violence and even murder.[1]

Noise—a word that is commonly defined as anything unwanted or even just an unpleasant sound—is now seen/heard to be a pollutant. As human beings are getting louder and louder, the world around us keeps step, but the natural world becomes more and more difficult to just hear, let alone listen to. As many external factors operate, we do not notice it except sporadically or when the level of sound becomes unbearable. Biologists are beginning to report that even birds and animals are beginning to suffer from the added, artificial noise—interrupting and silencing mating calls or the ability to sense all the other sounds of birds, mammals, reptiles, amphibians, even plants, trees, and ground covers. Bernie Krause, a musician and naturalist calls these human additions to the sound spectrum "anthrophony," saying that it disrupts the natural symphony and "causes the critters to have to find new bandwidths they can vocalize in and when they do that it becomes very chaotic and has a great impact on them and causes great stress."[2] And it is affecting marine animals, especially whales, dolphins, and all those sea creatures that rely heavily on sonar and highly developed hearing for following their migration patterns, communicating, and even sensing predators. Krause ends his piece by saying, "A great silence is spreading over the natural world even as the sound of man is becoming deafening."[3]

What are we to do in this world we are creating? Perhaps we are given a hint in the surprising knowledge of Beethoven, the marvelous composer who went deaf and never heard a note of his Ninth Symphony, along with so much of his repertoire. Do we have an internal system and capability of hearing and not-hearing, of choosing what we listen to and what we "mute"? There is an old Sufi story about an adept—as their teachers are often called—sitting on the deck of a ship. One of the passengers came upon him and all he could talk about was the noise—of the wind, the sea, the sailors, the creaking of the mast and the wooden hull, the groaning of the ship against the elements and the incessant noise of the crew yelling back and forth along with the other passengers throwing up, moaning, groaning, and everything on deck lurching to and fro. He kept complaining: "The noise! The noise! Will it never cease? Awful! Terrible! Shattering my eardrums! I can't hear myself think! Night and day—it's driving me mad!"

To his surprise, the adept answered him, saying, "Oh, I didn't notice it until you brought it to my attention." He continued, "When I want to hear it, I hear it, and when I don't want to hear it, I don't hear it." The man was stunned into silence! It is said that both of them could hear. Only one had the power and the sense of when and how to open or close it. The other had the door of his hearing open but hadn't yet thought or learned how to close it.

What if that is the case with all of us? What if we can—and must—learn what to hear and how to choose what to exclude from our perceptions, setting our own ears, minds, and souls to a wavelength or band of perception? First, we must educate ourselves and others with what is essential and vital—what must be heard, singled out, and listened to with body and soul. The poet Maya Angelou puts it succinctly:

> I would have my ears filled with the world's
> music....all the sounds of life and living.[4]

Ah! That's the *what*. What about the *how*? There is an old story told in many of the world's religious traditions. It is deceptively simple.

Once upon a time, a number of students were sitting and remembering their teacher, Rabbi Dov Ber, the Maggid of Mezritch, telling stories of what he did and what would startle them. There were things they never forgot and were still trying to figure out. One of the students asked, "Do you remember what the Rabbi would do every morning at dawn? Yes, he'd go down to the lakes and pond and stroll along listening to the frogs croak! The frogs! When we'd ask him why, he'd say, 'Don't forget that the Master of the Universe created everything as good, and created everything to give praise! Everything! From the lowliest to the loftiest, animate and inanimate—even the frogs. And I figure if I can learn the frog's song I can learn so, so many others that are odd, or strange, or discordant, or harsh, or rude, or incomprehensible, even ugly and disturbing. They remind me every morning to be "on guard" for all that I'm missing and unaware of as I live, and I begin by praying with them.'"

We begin by selectively listening to what are not our usual or common sounds and perceptions, singling them out, appreciating them, and seeking to hear and understand them—everything from peoples' sighing, coughing, and breathing to the sound of a crane swinging into a building, to the subway's whoosh before it arrives in the station, and the all too loud voice of someone in a seat next to us on their phone or plugged into their music so loud that we can hear what they're intent on listening to as well. Attentive sorting out and distilling—it is a new way of hearing and listening. We begin to fine-tune our ability to hear the music, the melody in everything, and then decide if we should add it to our "playlist" on a regular basis. We must learn the discipline of tuning-out, but we must be very careful not to assume that we know what needs to be discarded or ignored. The depth and range of revelation, of where we can learn wisdom, insight, and meaning, are far more extensive than we often decide is important for us in our small worlds.

I was once on a very shallow, large, and old boat in the South Pacific, traveling between one island and another, with young boys walking the outriggers. The boat was rocking and listing in the sea, and many were getting sick, heaving over the side. I asked one of the old men steering the boat if there was a way to avoid getting seasick. He laughed and said, "Oh, there are all sorts of 'remedies,' but none of them really work. But there is a trick to keep being balanced without that sense of being "at sea" or having no foundation. Just keep looking at the horizon—it seems the wider our outlook, the less what is immediately around us affects us negatively." I began to wonder, if it works for our eyes, what can it do for our ears as well? What if we reach with our ears as far as we can, straining for sound and stillness, can we sort out what we're hearing from a different range of what is important, or can we begin to hear differently and so hear underneath and through what is exteriorly just noise?

The Scriptures have stories of those born deaf being given the ability to hear, and those who have gone deaf learning to hear once again. They are very visceral stories of Jesus teaching others how to hear and what to do afterwards so that they won't go deaf again—on both a physical level and a level of spirit and humanness. This one is found in Mark.

> Again he left the district of Tyre and went by way of Sidon to the Sea of Galilee into the district of the Decapolis. And people brought to him a deaf man who had a speech impediment

and begged him to lay his hand on him. He took him off by himself away from the crowd. He put his finger into the man's ears, and, spitting, touched his tongue; then he looked up to heaven and groaned, and said to him, "*Ephphatha!*" (that is, "Be opened!") And [immediately] the man's ears were opened, his speech impediment was removed, and he spoke plainly. He ordered them not to tell anyone. But the more he ordered them not to, the more they proclaimed it. They were exceedingly astonished and they said: "He has done all things well. He makes the deaf hear and [the] mute speak." (Mark 7:31–37)

The account of the opening of the man's ears, which in turn, looses his tongue, is visceral, intimate, and even just the telling of the story evokes sensate reactions. It is worth noting that the story is initiated by others—some people, not named, bring the person to Jesus, not just to his attention but physically lead him into the physical presence of Jesus, and Jesus, in turn, takes him away from the crowd so that what transpires is just between the two of them, away from the eyes and ears of others. They begged him to "lay his hand on him"—more than just Jesus' taking him by the hand and bringing him off to a more private place.

The description of what Jesus does is stark and sensuous. He puts his fingers into the man's ears—holding his head between his hands and spitting, touched his tongue. Did Jesus' movement of putting his fingers into his ears cause him to open up his mouth? Did he spit onto the man's tongue? Then Jesus lifts his eyes to heaven and groans and then speaks aloud, in a sharp command: "Be opened!" In those few words, Jesus engages all of his own senses: touching, tasting, seeing, hearing, and smelling—to grasp and hold the man before him, concentrating everything on his head, face, and body, so intimate with him. We are told the reaction or response to Jesus' ministrations are *immediate*! This is one of Mark's favorite and often repeated words, meant to communicate the power of Jesus' actions and words as well as the gut reactions of the person he is engaged with so strongly. Jesus' touch, actions, and words trigger a series of reactions—the man's ears are opened, his tongue is loosed, and he speaks plainly. Three of his sensibilities have been restored to functioning and being expressed so that not only can he now understand others but others can now understand him.

Jesus' reaction to the outpouring of his strength and healing power into the man may seem strange—ordering them not to tell anyone and, of course, like people everywhere, they ignore the command and proclaim it all the more. They "proclaim" it—the action, and the result that is the effect of the good news of God in Jesus' presence and Jesus' abiding kingdom of wholeness, peace, and open and freeing relations among us. Why does Jesus not want them to tell anyone? Perhaps it's as simple as the need for the man to stop and become aware of his restored abilities and to use them with care and integrity. On Jesus' part, he does not want the healings—the effects of his presence—to be the focus of the attention and adulation, but he wants the man and those who brought him to lay hands on him to experience a depth and breadth of change in regard to their own hearing and speaking.

Are they hearing the Word of God and taking it to heart and, in turn, being transformed deep in their own lives, speech, dialogue, and relationships with others? The man who is deaf is each (and all) of us. There are people we are deaf to; there are things that we do and relationships that we are deaf to—refusing to listen and obey anyone who might try to approach us and get us to listen, to understand, and to respond—to them or to others. We are often unaware of how desperate others have become in relation to things we do and say, and how we live—wanting someone to get through to us, to change and transform the way we hear, listen, speak, and proclaim what we think or believe. We often forget or are totally unaware of how isolated and trapped inside our own heads, our own biases, and our own hearts we have become. We have no sense of the effect we have on others around us.

Such miracles as being able to hear and to speak plainly are not primarily meant to be physical altercations and changes. They are meant to reveal the presence and power of the Spirit to open our ears and hearts in such a way that we not only hear words but listen deeply to the presence of another person (and thus to God as well). Our ears are connected to our tongues and our ability to hear is strongly connected to our ability to speak plainly.

This entire chapter of Mark's Gospel is concerned with understanding. Just lines earlier, Jesus has been struggling to speak with the Pharisees, some scribes and elders of the Jewish community, and they are intent on doctrines, traditions, customary rules, and their own agendas rather than the teachings of the prophets and the commands of God. In speaking with them, Jesus quotes Isaiah the Prophet, calling them hypocrites: "This people honors me with their lips, but their hearts are far from me; in vain do they worship me, teaching as doctrines human precepts" (Mark 7:7). He rebukes him with hard words and examples of their own behavior—using their own words that give them influence over the people but, at the same time, lets them excuse themselves from obeying basic commands such as "Honor your father and mother." He accuses them bluntly:

> "You nullify the word of God in favor of your tradition that you have handed on. And you do many such things." [Then he summons the whole crowd—into the discussion, crying out to them:] "Hear me, all of you, and understand. Nothing that enters one from outside can defile that person; but the things that come out from within are what defile." (Mark 7:13–15)

Then we are told that they go home, away from the crowd, and he turns to his disciples and questions them: "Are even you likewise without understanding?" (Mark 7:18). How deaf are we to the essence and core of belief and practice? How deaf are we to the Word of God as the strongest words of how to live? Or do we have many "noisy" traditions framed historically that contradict point-blank the teachings and the practices of Jesus in the Gospels? How intent are we on making others agree with our interpretation of issues, events, and peoples' characters rather than hearing them in conjunction with God's listening to all of us? Do we hear only what we want to hear—only what backs up our own prior beliefs or what confirms our own way of being? How often do we need to be questioned: "Are even you likewise without understanding?" Jesus is intent on healing all of our faulty and blocked hearing as well as loosing our tongues so that we can speak plainly to one another. The specifics of ears and tongue are doorways into means of communicating with others with openness, carefulness, and clarity.

Someone (a rabbi in New York years ago) once told me that the opening phrase of prayer that we as Christians use, quoting a line from the Jewish Scripture: "Open our ears, O Lord, that we may hear your voice," (the word *voice* is sometimes translated "word") actually can be translated very differently—in a way we'd never forget. A translation that reveals the intent more clearly is "Drill a hole in our ears [heart], O Lord, so that we might hear your Word/Voice!" It seems our ears are connected directly to our hearts, and our hearts are as thick and hard as our ears are blocked and unhearing. Opening our ears and listening to everyone and everything is bound to the openness and acceptance of our hearts. For the majority of the world—all eastern and oriental peoples—the heart is the dwelling place of the will. So our ears begin the blockage that hardens our hearts and shuts down our will to respond and interact with others. There is an invisible triangle among our ears, heart, and tongue. They reinforce one another, and when there is need for change, any change, it must affect all three senses and parts of our personality and spirituality and practices of living.

Listening to noise, to what is unpleasant; to what and whom we disagree with; to what grates on us physically or annoys us psychologically; to all that we find disruptive and all that we judge wrong, harsh, or even evil is a necessity if we are to use our complete range of hearing and understanding. Revelation and truth reside in all sound whether we are attuned to glean it, draw it out, or not. If we cannot stop and practice the discipline of hearing underneath and through sound, including what we recoil from—then we will find that our hearts are hardening along with our minds and spirits shrinking up. This condition bleeds deeply into our ability to hear, to listen, and to understand and comprehend suffering, violence, disagreements, despair, loneliness, loss, isolation, injustice, and anything that batters the lives and persons of others.

There is a terrible story of sound, music, agony, praying, and pain that perhaps can say what cannot be said plainly. I call the story "Do You Hear What I Hear?" (like the Christmas carol). I heard it told only once, and I try to tell it rarely because of its power and destruction/ devastation as well as wisdom. Here are the basic bones of the story:

Once upon a time, the people of the synagogue were gathered on the holiest day of the year and their rabbi was praying. He was a great and holy man, and when he prayed they could trust and rely on him to gather their prayers together as one and bring them before the Holy One, blest be His Name. They waited for him to finish the prayers. Finally, he paused and they waited...and the pause seemed to drag on and on. Finally, he turned to the people and said, "I cannot say the prayers any longer. I do not have the strength. You know that when we come to pray before The Holy One, we must pray out loud and chant the words with such commitment that we are willing to die before the prayer is ended. I need someone to do that for me this day."

There was silence in the synagogue. The Rabbi turned again to them all and said, "Surely there is someone who is willing to sing the prayer, knowing it may be the last prayer and the last song you ever utter. Please." Then the people who were all seated heard a sound from the back of the room; it was a bench scraping. They all turned—in dismay—to see their old cantor rise and nod to the rabbi that he would do it. They were shocked—once this man had had a strong, clear superb voice, but over the years, it broke and he became hoarse, unable to hit notes or sustain a melody. No matter how bad it became, he forced himself to sing, and by the time he was made to step down, he had no voice. He rasped. The sound was guttural, or shrieking. He had no control over what sounds came forth from his mouth. It had been years since he had even tried to speak, let alone sing and cant.

He came forward and stood beside the rabbi and began. It was beyond terrible. People cringed at the sounds. He sounded like an animal growling, spitting, hissing, someone having trouble breathing. They could not understand one word of the prayer. Beside him, the rabbi groaned and moaned, crying and obviously in terrible distress and physical pain. Still the old man tore out the words in sounds that were scraping against the ears and souls of the people. The rabbi fell to his knees, and then as the wretched sounds continued, he fainted on the floor. The people didn't know what to do. They were concerned about their rabbi on the floor and the cantor's silences now except for bursts of ugly noises.

Finally, someone knelt beside the rabbi and touched his face gently asking, "Are you all right?" After a while, the rabbi opened his eyes and looked around at all of them bent over him with such concern. He sat up slowly and spoke: "Yes, thank you. If you hadn't touched me and spoken, I probably would have died." He stood slowly and put his arm around the old cantor's shoulders, then faced the group and said, "Thank you for praying with me and our cantor. I know you had to bring me back, or I never would have returned to you. But part of me also wishes you hadn't spoken or touched me." They looked at him still wondering how he was. Then he told them: "You see, in the terrible silences and, even more, in the awful sounds of this man's song, I heard the music of The Holy One." Then, the two of them, facing the congregation, picked up the prayer and continued. Now, they all prayed with such passion and sound that they had never experienced before—their voices singular and yet somehow altogether one in praise. They later said that they each heard the sound of

The Holy One in their ears and hearts and thrumming through their bodies, and they didn't die.

Sound, from one end of the spectrum of hearing and articulation is filled with revelation, with wisdom that can be drawn forth, that can be understood and transmitted plainly to others. We must dig deeply into all sounds as surely and deeply as we do into silences and learn not only to hear but to listen and stand inside and under sound. Do you hear what I hear? Are we listening to one another and the sounds of being human and what is buried within all life, being, and reality? *Listen Here!*

REFLECTIONS AND PRACTICES

1. Pick something to read to yourself—either something you are familiar with or a new piece—a story, a poem, or a portion of the Scriptures. Lay out the book or paper in front of you. Rest your arms, elbows bent on the table, and put your hands over your ears. Then read it out loud and listen to the sound of your voice in your ears. What do you sound like? Read it again out loud with your hands over your ears and listen, this time, for the content rather than the sound. Then read it a third time, without your hands over your ears. Do you hear and listen and perceive differently?

2. Pick a piece of your favorite music, pick another piece that you are not familiar with, and another that you know you're not keen on listening to—

what you consider noise, not music. Listen to them first with earphones on and then with your ears. Notice the volume—how much does the volume change with the three pieces? Do you prefer listening with your ears or through headphones? What does that tell you about yourself?

3. Spend a day or an evening noting down, as you go through your usual activities, two lists—of what you consider noise: unpleasant, jarring, or discordant—and of what you consider musical, engaging, uplifting, and freeing. Then take some time and see what the differences are—and what they call forth in you. Then do it with others and talk about it so that you learn from listening to others sense of what is noise and what is music.

In memory everything seems to happen to music.

—Tennessee Williams

7

LISTENING WITH HOPE

I raise up my voice—not so that I can shout, but so that those without a voice can be heard.

—Malala Yousafzai

It is crucial too that we keep remembering that negotiations, peace talks, forgiveness and reconciliation happen most frequently not between friends, not between those who like one another. They happen precisely because people are at loggerheads and detest one another as only enemies can. But enemies are potential allies, friends, colleagues, and collaborators.

—Desmond Tutu

Listening is hard. It is always hard. But there are myriad circumstances that make listening even more difficult: a work to be engaged in faithfully, with hope and with determination. There are so many of these realities where listening seems fruitless, exhausting, and of no consequence. The litany can go on and on: death, violence, suffering, hatred, torture, war and all its aftermath, personal hostilities, feuds, vendettas, rivalries, experiences of injustice, humankind's seemingly endless ability to hurt and destroy other human beings, and structural injustices such as human trafficking, slavery, poverty that are the result of harsh capitalism and greed, and the lives of so many that are dragged daily through despair, isolation, imprisonment, and a sense of worthlessness. Listening in these situations is a discipline, a gift in communicating, and a necessity of life that must be left open to possibilities—of forgiveness, restitution, reconciliation, the telling of the truth, and the restoration of relationships—in a word—to a *future* of life, life ever more abundant and inclusive.

We ended the last chapter listening to music and dissonance, and perhaps we can pick up there and yet reach forward in hope to the creation of possibilities for all in these situations and relationships. The following story is often called simply "The Bell." I was given the children's book decades ago, but it was lost as I moved around. I remember the author's name—Lee Oo Chung—and that the title was *The Emille Bell.* This is how I tell it:

Once upon a time, there was an ancient temple that had a bell that was renowned for its exquisite sound. People would come from all over the country to sit and wait and listen for its tones on the air and let it sound deep within their own bodies and ears. They say that it had been built by the ancients because the leader's advisors had counseled him to have a bell crafted in honor of the Buddha. It would allow the people to demonstrate their honor of the Buddha, and it was believed by the advisors who had studied traditions that the bell would keep the country safe and secure from invasion. The larger the bell, the stronger and more pervasive that protection would be.

And so, the king commissioned the bell makers in the land to make bells. They made many of all sizes, with tones that were as varied as their size, construction, and materials. Most were pleasant sounding. One or two had a tone that was different, that made you want to hear it again, but if the truth be told, none of them were extraordinary or remarkable for their tone. The king grew frustrated and annoyed and demanded that his counselors give him more information on what was necessary to make the bell sound exquisite, exceptional, and singularly unique in all the world. They went back to their books and queried the bell makers on any traditions that they were aware of—on how to change the tone of the bell so that it produced a singularly deep, light, free, and inspiring sound.

From all their study and research, there emerged one suggestion—that was horrible, inhuman, and destructive. But they all agreed—to alter the bell's tone, it was necessary that at a precise moment in the mixing of the metals, a young girl must be sacrificed and dropped into the molten liquid. This was the necessary missing ingredient if the bell were to be one of a kind. The king did not hesitate. Immediately, he sent his soldiers out to find a young girl child. They didn't go far. A mother and her daughter were on their way to town for market day, an outing they had just begun to share together. The young child was seized and dragged away from her mother. The soldiers were heedless of her mother's cries of despair and shock and the child's whimpering and fear.

The young girl kept crying out, "Emille! Emille! Emille—mother o mother!" but she was ignored. The mother followed, seeking a way to get to her child and save her, but to no avail. At the proscribed moment when the iron and molten lead were being blended together, the young girl was hurled into the huge mixture. Her cries were stopped. This time the bell maker succeeded. The bell, when rung, was beyond description.

The bell was christened "The Emille Bell" and its sound was light and deep. It lingered in the air, hanging as though it was trying to touch everyone's ears and their very souls. When it was rung, people stopped, arrested by its sound. They would barely breathe, swallowing its tone as it drifted and disappeared into the air. They would sigh and turn silently back to their tasks or try to speak and praise the bell and its maker; all but the child's mother and the few who knew the terrible truth—when they heard it ring, tears coursed down their faces, they had lumps rise in their throats, and their hearts broke again and again. There were so few who knew the story and the reason for the bell's sound. They carried the pain, the violence, the disregard for human life, the sacrifice, and the destruction of the young girl and her mother close and shuddered when the bell was tolled. Only those who knew the violence and understood the suffering could feel the pain that sources such grief. All the others only heard and enjoyed the sound.

It is a devastating story. I distinctly remember seeing "For Ages 3–8" printed on the inside cover. It haunts. It questions. It demands. It makes one sick and angry. It cannot be forgotten. So it is a story that introduces us to the harshness of the undertone and undercurrent that can bring forth sound. It is found in words, in moans and cries, grieving, sobs, awful noises that are torn from throats and hearts, and in silence that screams. It is the foundation and pattern of so many experiences, relationships, and circumstances of human living and interactions.

Writing about it doesn't do it justice, but all great writing seeks to put it into words, describe its power, and share it with others so that it can be heard, absorbed, taken to heart, and integrated into our lives with one another. This kind of writing is a form of resistance and of hope in the midst of despair and an invitation to open the dialogue that is a necessity for people to continue to live, not merely survive or to destroy themselves and everything around them. I was reading what I call "throwaway" literature—medieval murder mysteries of England—and I was stunned by the opening paragraph of one of these stories.

It began, as the greatest of storms do begin, as a mere tremor in the air, a thread of sound so distant and faint, yet so ominous, that the ear that was sharp enough to catch it instantly pricked and shut out present sounds to strain after it again, and interpret the warning. Brother Cadfael had a hare's hearing, readily alerted and sharply focused. He caught the quiver and bay, at this point surely still on the far side of the bridge that crossed the Severn from the town, and stiffened into responsive stillness, braced to listen.[1]

When I first read it, I thought it was the description of a storm since it was in the deep of night around the time of Matins. I had fleetingly thought it might be describing an account of a hunt, with the horses/men and dogs in pursuit but soon realized it wasn't because of timing. But in a sense, it was the introduction to some of both realities—it was the hunting of a man by a mob that was drunk and intent on killing the poor terrified person whom they had decided was a thief and a murderer. He was racing for the church sanctuary with every ounce of his strength to save his life. (It turned out that he wasn't either, only an innocent and poor wanderer caught in the wrong place and easily blamed, who would have been hung and beaten to death literally by a "good, self-righteous and very drunk Christian mob.")

Listening in many situations and relationships is just such a storm that can suck many into an eddy that can destroy quickly and only exacerbate the situation and confuse the reality that provoked the storm. There are always two sides (at least) to every encounter, injustice, and what is perceived as the "right" response to all situations and trigger points of experience. The first stance of anyone who listens must be to choose to listen to all sides and yet to choose to listen standing between and in the midst of all parties. Harder still, we must choose to listen more closely and openly to the one who is the victim, the one not listened to, the one blamed, and the one who is the focus of rage, hurt, violence, murderous intent, and suffering. This is how Elie Wiesel, recipient of the Nobel Prize for Peace explained his stance:

> I always try to listen to the victim. In other words, if I remain silent, I may help my own soul but, because I do not help other people, I poison my soul....Indifference means there is a kind of apathy that sets in and you no longer appreciate beauty, friendship, goodness, or anything—so therefore do not be insensitive....Be sensitive, only sensitive. Of course, it hurts. Sensitivity is painful. So what? Think of those that you have to be sensitive to. Their pain is greater than yours.[2]

> This sentiment, this determination and discipline is echoed by many others, among them some of the human beings who have been strongest in their pursuit of the truth and reconciliation and justice for all, but most especially for the stranger, the outsider, the victim, the one most easily ignored and silenced.[3]

Martin Luther King Jr. said, "Our lives begin and end the day we become silent about things that matter." The work, the art, the discipline is three-fold: *Listen*, abide in the silence, and *Decide* whether or not to respond, then *Stand* with the truth, whether it is with words, with solidarity, or with resistance. But each of us must choose. This is the way another rabbi put it in a speech that immediately preceded Martin Luther King's closing address at the American Jewish Congress.

> When I was the rabbi of the Jewish community in Berlin under the Hitler regime, I learned many things. The most important thing that I learned under those tragic circumstances was that bigotry and hatred are not the most urgent problem. The most urgent, the most disgraceful, the most shameful and the most tragic problem is silence.[4]

To speak about listening in conflict, in dialogue, in the making of peace and reconciliation, of stemming the tsunami of violence, the first step is listening, but it is yoked to responding and coming forth from silence that is deadly when it serves to escalate any situation or allows others to suffer. Elsa Tamez, a theologian from Central America, posits that God is silent—but for a reason that we must heed and respond to if we are to remain human, let alone be made in the image of our God.

> God remains silent so that men and women may speak, protest and struggle. God remains silent so that people may really become

people. When God is silent and man and
women cry, God cries in solidarity with them
but doesn't intervene. God waits for the shouts
of protest.[5]

This is where we must become human beings and
make sure that we are listening to those who are not
being heard and share our voice with theirs. Arundhati
Roy, a woman writer in India has said it over and over
again, very clearly—"There's really no such thing as the
'voiceless'. There are only the deliberately silenced, or
the preferably unheard." In so much of our lives, we are
summoned to hear and listen to those among us that
seek to be heard and to speak. We must connect to them.
We must stand with them. We must listen to them—it is
a form of prayer, a way of meditating so that we can
mediate with them, and for them with others.

Somehow we must learn the net of listening—
beyond our own small connections or agenda to a wider
and wider sphere of influences and relationships. It is in
a way, a listening in the place where we are all one in
our common humanness. Among the Lakota peoples
(mainly in North and South Dakota) there is a phrase
Mitaksuye Oyasin that is usually translated, "all my relations," reminding everyone that we are all bound as one,
together, each of us interconnected to all others, responsible with all and fundamentally one. When they greet
one another or part from one another, they do not say
things like "How are you?" or, "What's up?" or, "Have a
good day." Instead they say, *Tza Nee da Bee Wah*, which
is usually translated as "How are your connections?" or

"How are your relations?" (That includes all humans but also everything else that is created.) For the Lakota and many other Native peoples, every single human being is sacred and has power, influence, and insight—blessed by the Spirit and that must be honored all ways. This kind of listening is communion. The differences and gaps remain, but they can be bridged and there can be movement back and forth from both directions.

Perhaps we all need to be taught some basics once again. For instance, we could begin with just being with others, especially anyone we perceive to be other—or different—or strange, dangerous, not like us. This is the case for all of us with individuals, but it is also the reality of whole groups of people, nations, races, those of other faiths, economic brackets, tribes, and sides within families. Someone sent me this great picture of porcupines that I keep on my wall in the room where I write. I often have seen folks trap one (and have done it myself when needed to keep the creatures from chewing the bark of tender trees). A big trash can or barrel is dropped over the creature. It doesn't get harmed but it shoots its spines and needles out into the enclosure. Then you carefully knock over the enclosure so they can escape—and then go to collect all the spines—carefully! Many of my Native friends use them for making earrings and for decorating and embroidering their clothes and capes. But you have to be extremely careful. The spines are painful and hard to remove from skin. The person who sent me the photograph also included an amazing quote from Arthur Schopenhauer.

On a cold winter's day a group of porcupines crowded together to keep each other warm, and save themselves from freezing to death. But the feel of each other's prickles made them separate. When their need for warmth brought them together again, the sensation was repeated. So it went on until they found the distance away from each other where they could best endure the situation.

This distance we recognize as courtesy and good manners.[6]

So simple! So necessary! So worth remembering! So essential to learn to practice and keep in mind for all of us. This is a starting point—carefulness of others as we all share the same humanity, weaknesses and strengths, space and time on this earth.

This way of listening is intent on openness, acceptance, seeking what unites and what we share, opening doors wherever possible. It is born of creativity, shared dignity, imagination, and all that gives and deepens life. It entails learning to listen together, with others and to others, suspending judgments and refraining from demands but knowing that restoration and compromise, justice and forgiveness are building blocks of conversations and sharing life together—in food and meals, gifts, prayer, silence, music and art, and especially in telling one another stories and histories to begin to build upon in the present, instead of being trapped in perceptions and realities of the past. Places like Taizé in France (an ecumenical monastic community founded by Brother

Roger) draw together people from every religion, praying in silence, in music, and in worship together. Another such place is Thich Nhat Hahn's mindfulness community in France that brings people together in shared mediation, silence, walks, and the everyday chores of feeding, cooking, cleaning, and housing many visitors as well as the community that welcomes and hosts others in a spirit of peace that is more than coexistence. It leans toward life-giving work for peace and truth-telling that models how it's done and what it looks like for anyone to see.

Religion is one starting place, but there must be spaces and times to listen to those aggrieved, broken, and treated violently, to speak, and to be heard by the larger world so that nations, leaders, and all peoples can learn to listen to others and to respond more humanly. There are places everywhere in the world to start—perhaps one such group of places would be wherever there are walls. There is an amazing piece by Eduardo Galeano simply titled "Walls" that can open some doors for what needs to be done and where and how to do it.

> The Berlin Wall made the news every day. From morning till night we read, saw, heard: the Wall of Shame, the Wall of Infamy, the Iron Curtain...
>
> In the end, a wall which deserved to fall fell. But other walls sprouted and continue sprouting across the world. Though they are much larger than the one in Berlin, we rarely hear of them.

Little is said about the wall the United States is building along the Mexican border, and less is said about the barbed-wire barriers surrounding the Spanish enclaves of Ceuta and Melilla on the African coast.

Practically nothing is said about the West Bank Wall, which perpetuates the Israeli occupation of Palestinian lands and will be fifteen times longer than the Berlin Wall. And nothing, nothing at all, is said about the Morocco Wall, which perpetuates the seizure of the Sharan homeland by the kingdom of Morocco, and is sixty times the length of the Berlin Wall.

Why are some walls so loud and others mute?[7]

These are walls made of stone, mortar, boards, concrete blocks, pieces of tin, but there are walls of silence, of memory, of words, even music and prayers that divide, separate, isolate, and feed hate. All need dismantling. The African writer Chinua Achebe said, "As long as people sit on another and are deaf to their cry, so long will understanding and peace elude all of us."

Where do we begin? How do we start? I think we start with hope. When I was in South Africa, I heard a woman talking about hope in one of the townships, and I've never forgotten something she said—you have to learn to wear hope like a second skin. The women I was with talked about that—it can be pierced, punctured, and it can hurt. It has to be tough enough to take some bruising but still retain its sensitivity and feeling. This

skin is meant for touching, knowing weathers of sun
and rain but also embracing and holding on to others.
Hope is always about connecting with others, especially
those you have had bad experiences with or memories
that you both want to forget and can't forget. This skin
is about restoring confidence, about taking risks, about
facing the future, while you keep bits of the past in
reserve and use only as needed. Like hope, this skin has
to be constantly mended, kept in good repair so that it
can be reused again and again.

Later, I remembered a word from Mexico I learned
on one of my first visits. I was watching a woman weave
on a back strap loom strung between two trees. She was
weaving and talking to me, and her young son was also
weaving on his little loom. She seemed never to drop a
stitch while her child's piece was filled with knots and
dropped stitches. Every fifteen minutes or so, she'd stop
her work and sit beside him on the ground and carefully
keep talking—to me and to him—and unravel all the mis-
takes, going back to the first dropped thread and reknot-
ting it. She never disparaged his weaving and instead
said things like, "Oh, that's so different," or, "I will have
to try putting those two colors together on mine." I was
trying to learn words from her and asked her a word to
explain the tangled threads and what the backside of her
weaving looked like. One of the words she used was
enredo, and she said the word was used for other things
too—the fishermen used it to describe their nets when
they came in from fishing—tangled and torn from everything they had snagged, besides fish. The nets were
mostly the color red, though there were some green ones

too. She then mentioned that it was the word they used when there was conflict in the village and the people needed to get together to unravel situations that had developed or just untangle the mess of people's relationships that were affecting others. I couldn't help but remember Jesus' parable about the kingdom of God—the relationships between those in his community, with God, and with all others too.

> Again, the kingdom of heaven is like a net thrown into the seas which collects fish of every kind. When it is full they haul it ashore and sit down to put what is good into buckets. What is bad, they throw away. (Matt 13:47–48)

The image is concise and full of insight. There are frequent references to the fisherman daily "putting their nets in order" or "mending their nets" or "washing their nets" after a long night or early morning session of fishing (see Mark 1:19; Luke 5:2). It is an innate part of the process, as preparation and repair each time they went out to fish. The men and women weave and fish on land and sea, and they use this work as time for reflection, discernment, and figuring out how to live into the future and repair anything that might be a problem in the community's relationships and smooth operation. This has to become our own daily process as individuals, as families, communities, even as nations. This is as much the making of hope, the repairing of the second skin, as anything that might take place with others when we are intent on making peace, reconciling, listening, and

doing justice, restoring the fabric of our political, economic, religious, national, and international lives.

We live with others and invariably we must learn
to repair the world and our relationships with others.
Porcupines, walls and weavings, fishing and befriending
others are all of a piece, following many of the same patterns. Becoming whole, or holy, cannot be regulated to
the individual, but we must become who we are with
others and perhaps begin with the premise that becoming whole is done for others too. What follows is wisdom
from our elders, those who lived on this land before we
arrived. It is wisdom that is found among many peoples.

> In all your deliberations, in your efforts at law
> making, in all your official acts, self-interest
> shall be cast into oblivion. Cast not over your
> shoulder behind you the warnings of the
> nephews and nieces should they chide you for
> any error or wrong you may do, but return to
> the way of the Great Law which is just and
> right. Look and listen for the welfare of the
> whole people and have always in view not
> only the present but also the coming genera-
> tions, even those whose faces are yet beneath
> the surface of the ground—the unborn of the
> future nation.[8]

We begin by remembering who we are as belonging
to others, in communion with others, and from there
reach out, and we become more aware of still others
beyond our usual circles. We must listen to others tell

their stories, explain their positions, and even defend their principles. We need to start always at the beginning—to sound through others, catching some sense of their persons and being and how they live on earth, like us, with us, and yet different than us. In the words of Howard Thurman, "In the stillness of the quiet, if we listen, we can hear the whisper of the heart giving strength to weakness, courage to fear, hope to despair." Just listening can alleviate a great deal of another's pain, insecurity, and fear. First listen, then recognize difference, then celebrate it! Audre Lorde, a black woman poet, essayist, and a voice for justice and truth, reminds us of the power of our differences—they are not to be ignored, changed, or gotten rid of: "It is not our differences that divide us. It is our ability to recognize, accept, and celebrate those differences."

Differences do not have to be problematic or even sources of fear, anger, or division. We can communicate and relate in spite of them, through them, over them, around them, and under them. There is an amazing story told by Richard M. Kelly in an article he wrote for *Friends Journal* titled "Truth as a Moving Target on a Local Train." He tells the story to many groups in many situations. The backdrop to the story is a train ride in July 1979 going from Geneva to Basel. The train is packed with people, with noise, litter, spirited conversation, sweat, and children. He begins by describing two middle-aged Jewish men sitting across the aisle from him, jackets off, but their hats still on. They were hot, like everyone else in the train car, and sweat poured down from their yarmulkes and beaded on their lips. This is how the story continues, in his words:

> Open copies of a book in Hebrew, likely the Talmud, were on their laps. They argued back and forth with great agitation and enthusiasm; sometimes pointing to the text, sometimes at each other. Sometimes their gestures simply punctuated the humid air in the crowded train. I understood none of their words.
>
> After some time observing what I did not understand, I realized that I had missed one of the most interesting features of their conversation. One of the men was speaking French; the other was speaking German!
>
> What a metaphor I thought for the confusion we have in life. Here were two, obviously intelligent, educated and passionate adults, arguing with one another in two different languages about the meaning of a third language. Here am I, limited to English. Where would anyone find the Truth in that scenario?[9]

The story is magnificent! In fact, it is a story inside a story inside yet another story. The first is the scene in the train with the two men in the midst of chaos, being observed by another man, and the amazing reality of their differences in languages, religion, and nationalities. The second story is when he tells it as indicative of many situations and relationships we each experience in our own lives. The third story is that it can serve as a

metaphor and process of how all people live and interact with one another, often unaware of or in spite of
major differences, lacks, and (sometimes) severely limiting points of view and ways of communicating. In all
the stories, there are hidden treasures, bits of wisdom
that we can glean in our own seeking to listen in communion with others.

What draws the two men together in the midst of
their different languages is a third party—in this case, a
common shared bond to a tradition—the Talmud that is
written in another language both knows. Along with
that shared book, there is shared respect, appreciation of
the dignity of the other, and an acceptance that both
have something to say, something to listen to, and
something that might be of meaning to the other. All situations must begin with this and it must be maintained
in the heat of argument, anger, or hurt.

The observer, while not participating in the conversation or knowing either language or the meanings of
the Talmud's tradition, is drawn in by the passion and
intense focus in the midst of all the other confusion and
life around them. He is listening and it takes him a good
while to realize even the obvious—that they are not
speaking the same language and he knows neither of the
languages either. He knows them by sound in his ears
that is connected to what he is seeing. Our ears are connected to our eyes, and our ears are connected to our
hearts. In every human encounter, there is much to
see/hear/internalize/listen to in communion and then
absorb into our own lives and minds. There is no place
or interaction where revelation and wisdom cannot be

found—for those who have ears to hear and eyes to see and a heart that is open and responsive (to echo Jesus' words about his stories and parables in speaking with his followers).

The writer uses the image of the local train, a moving, passing train, and wonders if that is the way Truth operates and is known and perceived. We all must keep moving in a sense and not get stymied and stuck in whatever belief, assumption, bias, or a small truth that we use to define ourselves and those we have aligned ourselves with to live within our worlds. We have to continuously adapt and adjust our sense of what is truth to the larger realities of truth outside and beyond us. Each of us only has a taste of the truth, a glimpse of truth that we have experienced or taken within us to help us define our lives.

The Jewish *Pirkei Avot* (The Ethics of the Fathers) reminds us that the word *sage* (in Latin, *sapere*) means "to taste"! Each of us has a taste of the world and of wisdom, and there is a feast awaiting us everywhere and in everyone. There is a saying in Costa Rica: "Every word has three explanations and three interpretations." This is a feast that both adds to the taste and can confuse the palate too. Barbara Deming puts it this way: "The longer we listen to one another, with real attention, the more commonality (community) we will find in all our lives." It is always another, others that teach us to listen. Those who are "not like us" are our true mentors and teachers in this discipline.

Just as we learn to listen from others, we also can get stuck with others in refusing to listen and go deaf.

The company we keep can either hinder us or help us develop listening skills. There is a story told in a number of the Gospels that shares with us delight and imagination and determination of a group trying to help a friend and the opposite—a group that is solidly against listening to others, entrenched in their own ideas, and intent on keeping that wall up between themselves and others. Listen!

> When Jesus returned to Capernaum after some days it became known that he was at home. Many gathered together so that there was no longer room for them, not even around the door and he preached the word to them. They came bringing to him a paralytic carried by four men. Unable to get near Jesus because of the crowd, they opened up the roof above him. After they had broken through, they let down the mat on which the paralytic was lying. When Jesus saw their faith, he said to the paralytic, "Child your sins are forgiven." (Mark 2:1–5)

This is the set-up and backdrop. There is a huge crowd and no way to enter and push through to get near the presence of Jesus. But that doesn't stop the man's friends. They get on the roof, take out some of the tiles, removing a segment of the roof, and lower the man down right in front of Jesus. Such ingenuity! (Though one wonders what the owner of the house might think about the hole in his roof!) They have to use their creativity, their strength, and the existing conditions to get through to Jesus. They don't have to say anything. Jesus "hears" their care and compassion, their need, and is delighted with their wordless speaking on behalf of their friend. What we might find surprising is Jesus' verbal response when they silently lower their paralytic friend in front of him. But Jesus' response is not just for the man in need, or his friends, but for the crowd around him, and a group that is sitting before him, not listening to anything he is saying.

> "Child, your sins are forgiven." Now some of the scribes were sitting there asking themselves, "Why does this man speak that way? He is blaspheming. Who but God alone can forgive sins?" Jesus immediately knew in his mind what they were thinking to themselves, so he said, "Why are you thinking such things in your hearts? Which is easier, to say to the paralytic, 'Your sins are forgiven,' or to say, 'Rise, pick up your mat and walk'? But that you may know that the Son of Man has authority to forgive sins on earth"—he said to the paralytic, "I say to you, rise, pick up your mat, and go home." He rose, picked up his mat at once, and went away in the sight of everyone. They were all astounded and glorified God saying, "We have never seen anything like this." (Mark 2:5–12)

We are told the story in such a way that we can "listen" to Jesus' words, just as the paralytic, his friends who have brought him near to Jesus, the crowd, and as the group of scribes hears them, though the last sit watching what is going on, seeing and hearing, but never listening to Jesus—and probably not to anyone like the paralytic or his friends and most of the crowd too. Jesus listens to them in their thoughts and hearts as intently as he listens silently to the man's suffering and distress and the man's friends who are so careful of him and hoping for a better life for him. The crowds listen as well—some hearing only the words that are spoken, others to the underlying dissent between the scribes and Jesus and to the tensions in the crowd, taking sides also.

What Jesus says doesn't seem to be connected to the man's plight or his friends' hope for healing. But the two are intimately intertwined. Anyone who listens to us recreates us, gives birth to us, sets us free, heals us, and gives us a sense of future, possibilities, and hope. The man is paralyzed. In this case, he cannot move or walk. He is "stuck" here, but all of us get stuck. All of us need not only someone to listen to us, but others to give us a future and recreate us. Perhaps those who do it most attentively and consistently are those we call friends. The word *hope* comes from an Indo-European root word meaning "to expand" or "to stretch." Listening plants the seed of hope in another so that they can stretch into new areas of life, reach and try something new, or expand their consciousness and sense of themselves, setting them free. Even being told that we are forgiven sets us free and releases us from being imprisoned in something in the past that can paralyze us and keep us from living with gracefulness and gratitude.

Listening, accepting, and being forgiven can release us from so many debilitating consequences of what we have done and open us up to ways of acting that can redeem and heal relationships and situations.

Jesus is trying to do that to the man physically paralyzed but also trying to get the scribes unstuck from their confining ways of imprisoning people and being intent on keeping them there, paralyzed—rather than seeking to live and interpret their beliefs in such a way that others are freed and given hope. Jesus' words: "What is easier"—to give a person legs to stand on and walk or to give a person hope, setting them free to live and to live helping others to be evermore alive and in communion with others like the men who lowered their friend through the roof? What is the deeper and more powerful *miracle* (a word that means "a marvelous thing to behold")?

Listening with hope; listening for communion—done primarily in groups and in dire situations with others in pain, in violence, in fear, and in long-standing relationships of suffering and death—is a power and a skill that we must grow into, struggle to do, and learn with others. It is the essence of being a peacemaker, one who creates futures and life out of death and despair. Listening with hope, listening in hope is the foundation of our future together. It must be a priority in our lives and what we teach our children. Abraham Lincoln said, "Do I not destroy my enemies when I make them my friends?" Listening with hope is this process of making all of us friends. More than a practice, it must become our way of life. *Listen Here!*

REFLECTIONS AND PRACTICES

1. "The world is delicate and as complicated as a spider's web. If you touch one thread you send shudders through all the other threads. We are not just touching the web, we are tearing great holes in it" (Gerard Durrell). Try to draw a map of the country you live in and put an X where someone you know lives. Then add in stories or people from the news. Then with another color add in where people live who have done what you think are terrible things. Do you know of anyone who is listening to all sides? What does it mean to be a bridge between people who are so separated?

2. Make a list of what you don't want to hear about or people you don't want to have to relate to. What can you do when these issues or stories arise? Ask some of your friends and family and members of your communities that you live, work, and pray with what they do in such situations.

3. People who stand in between individuals and groups, even nations, and try to listen to both sides are called peacemakers—in the Gospels, Jesus calls them the children of God. Who do you see and hear in your life that is a peacemaker, listening and seeking to get others to listen to one another? If you have trouble finding someone like that in your world, begin to pray for peacemakers to come forward and help people listen to one another.

8

LET THERE BE NIGHT!

Listening to the Dark

We are as owls before the Light of God.
—Thomas Merton

*The real meaning of enlightenment is to
gaze with undimmed eyes on all darkness.*
—Nikos Kazantzakis

Since I was small I have loved the dark, the night, shadows, and the times in between as the day departed and as night left us. I remember nights in New York when I would lie outside on the ground lost in the dark above me, and night after night, I would watch and learn how the stars, the constellations, and the moon made of night a time of wonder and awe, learning old and new knowledge. Early on, I thought that the stars were tiny windows that opened onto our world for whoever was "up and out there" to peer through and see us with their eyes. Without being able to put it into words, I knew that it was the light that needed the darkness in order to exist. Without night and darkness, there was no meaning to light or day. I never understood why so many people were afraid of the dark. As I grew older, I could not easily accept that so much of literature, prayers, spirituality, and general expression seemed to associate darkness and night with something wrong, less than its counterpart light, even evil or something to endure or eliminate.

That coldest and darkest part of the night before dawn has been the deepest and most expansive time. It has always been so. In the East this time is called the Hour of the Tiger, the time to face fears, one's own shortcomings and vulnerability, as well as mortality. The Church of both the East and the West rises for Matins, the longest prayer of the twenty-four-hour cycle of praise and attentiveness to the Holy. The season of Advent instills in us a hunger for the night; for it is in the heart of darkness that the One long awaited will be born among us. For iconographers, night is the time for deep reflection and prayer when one bends over the icon and writes anew the presence of God's glory and humanity with us.

I resist labeling and the distortion that becomes permanent when what is dark and made of night is problematic—like "the dark night of the soul," or the judging of what is unknown, uncontrollable, or shrouded in mystery as tainted (the old catechism pictures of the *white* milk bottle and *dark* or *black* sin). This concept or belief leaked into so many things—races being more black than white—even today in the United States, if you

are one-sixteenth black, you are black. (The same goes
for equally small parts of Hispanic or Native American—
the standard being "white.") This dichotomy is limiting,
destructive, and does not express truths that are foundational to perceiving reality—on scientific or physical
levels, let alone psychological or more spiritual realities.

We need perhaps to go back to our beginnings
(Genesis) to look at some basics for many of us who are
Judeo-Christians. In the first of the creation stories, we
hear,

> When God began to create heaven and earth
> the earth being unformed and void, with dark-
> ness over the surface of the deep and a wind
> from God sweeping over the water God said,
> "Let there be light; and there was light. God
> saw that the light was good, and God sepa-
> rated the light from the darkness. God called
> the light Day, and the darkness He called
> Night. And there was evening and there was
> morning, a first day. (Gen 1:1–5)[1]

I chose a translation from the Jewish tradition
because, being more original as a source, it also is easier
to see the connections of how it is understood—which is
not always immediately apparent in other Christian versions. One of the first things that can arrest our attention
is that God is still creating and that God apparently
draws creation out of chaos—or elements that are primordial and trifold: earth that is unformed, darkness
over the surface of the deep, and a wind from God that

sweeps over the waters. God creates by word of mouth (so to speak), drawing forth from within God's self form, design, pattern, and order that is innate in what is made and continues and develops in existence, forever changing within the basic universe (one verse or song or expression). The pattern is "Let there be...," and something obeys and responds—or listens! This is followed by God seeing that it is good and God separating one thing from another, naming each and giving a description of the resultant reality (there are shifts and small discrepancies, but this is the basic pattern).

The first command uttered is "let there be light" and it is good and God separates light from the darkness. The separation is essential. Meaning is found in the relation to the other. Each is named—light is "Day" and darkness is "Night" and there is evening and morning and it is a first day. There is balance and harmony, a playing together, taking turns, following upon one another, a circular bent to time and space.

The question must be raised—what is this light that is created on the first day that is drawn forth from the darkness? As the story continues, what we commonly refer to as *light*—the physical and scientific realities of the sun, moon, and stars—bodies of energy in space, in the universe, are not summoned forth and named until the fourth day! So, what is this light? The answer is crucial because the answer removes the accrued dichotomy and judgmental appellations of good and evil from light and darkness. It is the belief and understanding of the Jewish tradition that this first "Let there be light" can be explained in a number of ways (midrash), the first being that God hid the first light or primordial light of his revelation and presence in the Torah and even in the Book of Creation to protect it and make it available to those who are righteous and just. Another midrash posits that this light was the summoning forth of each human soul held in the presence of God until they would be brought forth. And so, they and other ancient peoples refer to the sun, moon, stars, and planets as "luminaries" rather than "light." The sun and the moon are the greater light and the lesser light.

This is a very basic introduction to the cosmology of creation, but it can serve as a platform for separating out the simplistic rendering of good/evil and light/dark. There should not be/could not be and are not/were not any predications in regard to the realities of day and night or light and dark. These judgments and artificial characteristics are historically and culturally manmade, often in fear, ignorance, and simplistic ways of applying and speaking about "this" or "that," and need to be examined and altered—or at least given some subtlety, shadings, and balance. We need to start seeing and even hearing and sensing that the dark is good and light isn't always necessarily good, and they should be seen in relation to each other, listening to each and to both together.

We can start by remembering our own genesis—beginnings. We spend up to the first nine or ten months of our lives cushioned and bound to darkness in our mothers' wombs and are pulled and pushed out into the light. That gestation time is crucial to our physical well-being all our lives, and what transpires in that dark cocoon endows us with all our genetic material and the physical bodies that will continue the process of creation when we emerge and begin our lives on earth, in the day/night and light/darkness of this world. I have been told by a friend, who is a writer of icons, that the dark of night is the "right" time, the most fecund time to work on revealing and creating in light, color, and shadow/darkness something that speaks without words, but with sound of God who creates, sustains, and enlivens everything all ways, for all time.

Science too has lately "discovered" (in terms of actually getting a better understanding of) hidden and sometimes minimally understood details of how the universe was created and how it is still unfolding to become the reality we perceive. A friend, a monk and astronomer, once shared with me a huge coffee table–sized book of photographs taken by the Hubble Space Telescope over the last twenty plus years. It was beyond stunning and awesome—it revealed a world to me that I could never imagine, and it introduced me to a sense of scale, vastness, design that stretched whoever I thought God might be beyond what is individualistic or even a God in relation to humanity. It threw me once again (and again, and still does) into mystery that instills fear (that is holy and good), a need to worship beyond my own being in relation to the God who has summoned me forth into existence and hinted to hidden power and glory that now lingers on the edge of my consciousness, reminding me now and again that perhaps I really know very little of God.

About the Hubble Space Telescope, Carl Sagan said that the amount of data it has sent back to earth is so

mindboggling that they can barely keep up with cata-
loging it. But all the scientists in related fields have been
using the data to plot a map of the universe. They all
agree on one thing based on the information they have.
Staggeringly, they have found out that as much as 97.9
percent of the universe is invisible! From their plotting
of what they know/can see and their extrapolations,
their findings are consistent—what do we know of anything really?! My immediate reaction to this piece of
information was a gut reaction—what do we know of
God really?! Have we been shrinking our concept or
sense of God down to something that we can handle, try
to control, or think we understand? Are we afraid of
falling into the "hands of the living God," the mystery
of the universe and a God so beyond our reckoning that
we are only playing games with religion rather than
delving deeply into what it might actually mean to "be
made in the image and likeness" of this God?

Astronomers know now that our universe is expanding at an ever increasing rate, and they call the mysterious accelerant "dark energy." They know little about
it, but can see its effects and are intent on finding out
how galaxies are created, their beginnings—expanding and
in motion. They are continuing to map the universe, specifically from New Mexico over the Northern Hemisphere
with what is called BOSS, the Baryon Oscillation Spectroscopic Survey (due to be completed in June 2014).[2]
What they are mapping will give some hints and clues
as to the composition of the universe and how it is
expanding and maybe how this dark energy is pushing
it apart. This is just one small piece of what is being

relayed back to earth and to our computers and senses—along with such realities as dark matter, black holes, and so on. We are very new at knowing where we dwell, who we are, and who our God might be.

We must begin to realize and try to incorporate the concept that darkness is as the light is—a source of revelation and a holy reality. Darkness is fruitful, deep, the dwelling place of God, as essential to our maturation and development as light. Darkness is its own poetry, truth, and source of wisdom and freedom. Inspiration comes forth from darkness as surely as from the light of day and what it exposes. The hush, the emptiness, the void, the vastness, and the stillness/silence of night give birth to our senses, our spirit, and our souls as much as sleep renews and refreshes our bodies. We need first to embrace darkness and night and then to learn to go in search of it—beyond just day and night, into the unknown that beckons to draw us out and beyond—the horizon of the darkness as strong as any horizon sought in daylight.

Rachel Naomi Remen, a doctor and counselor, teacher and healer, has a story that starts with this sense of darkness, of night/day, and what darkness has all too often meant to us—something to be feared, pushed aside, ignored, or hidden. It is found in one of her books, *Kitchen Table Wisdom.* She tells it in the first person, based on an experience she had as a young child living in a walk-up flat in New York City. Her parents are both doctors also at the center of a fledging group of Jewish people intent on securing a state for Israel after World War II. They are Jewish, but not necessarily practicing religiously. They are more intent on Zionism and living after the Holocaust. Her grandfather, though, is one of the leading rabbis in the city and has a strong influence on her as a child. That influence emerges later in life as she lives and struggles with Crohn's disease and many operations as well as being a doctor herself.

This is the way I tell it, and I call it "Dark Pieces":

It was winter and I was in the living room. It was evening, and there was a stream of visitors that would come in the front door (always open) and down the long hallway into the kitchen where the adults would sit around the table and drink coffee and something stronger that made them talk louder and get more enthusiastic or subdued. There was something different though tonight. My father had set up a card table in the hallway and had left something on it, and everyone who came in stopped awhile and bent over it. They'd sometimes laugh or talk to themselves, stay awhile, and then go on down into the kitchen. The next morning after my father had gone to work and my mother was cleaning the kitchen, I pulled a chair into the hallway and got up to look at this "thing" that everyone was so interested in.

I didn't like it. There were pieces scattered all over the table. There were a lot of dark pieces: gray, black, black and blue—all of them ugly. There were a few pieces that had some red in them or maybe silver gray and even a few with something like yellow or gold, but too many black ones. There was a box but it was empty, and even the part that showed was dark gray. I decided to take some of the dark ones—and I grabbed a handful, got down from the chair, went and put them under the cushions in the sofa, and then dragged the chair back into the living room. It made me feel better—I'd gotten rid of some of the dark. Every morning, I'd take a few more pieces and hide them in the sofa.

But things began to change. All the people would come to talk with my parents, and they'd stop at the card table and bend over it and move things around. But now, they didn't laugh—though they did keep talking to themselves. In fact, now they were sometimes saying things that I'd been told never to say, and I wondered if I should tell papa what they were doing. Sometimes they'd even slam their fist down on the table or kick the wall. Now I was sure—I didn't like this thing with all its dark pieces.

Then one morning when I was bent over the table and about to take my pieces to put in the sofa, mama came out and asked, "Rachel, what are you doing?" My answer was, "Nothing." She looked at me and asked, "Rachel, do you know what this is?" My answer was, "No, and I don't like it—look at how dark and ugly it is." Mama laughed and said, "Rachel, this is your Papa's birthday present to me. It's called a jigsaw puzzle." I screwed up my face and said again, "I don't like it." Mama laughed and pulled over another chair, "Let's look at it and play with it together." Then she took the empty box and flipped it over. There was a beautiful picture on the box of the sun coming up on the beach! "Oh, that's just like the beach we go to sometimes—I love going." "Yes," said Mama, "and that's what all these pieces will look like, when we get them all together." "Ohhh, I don't see how. It's all too dark, and I've been watching and listening to people—they don't like it either. They say bad things when they're looking at this, and they kick the wall and aren't supposed to." Mama laughed again and said, "Well, that's because we're having trouble putting the pieces together. When we first started, it was fun and we remembered doing this when we were little like you, but lately it's become harder and harder, and we just can't seem to put it together."

She paused and then looked at me funny and said, "Rachel Naomi, is there anything you'd like to tell me?" My answer was a slow, "No." Mama kept looking at me, "Are you sure?" I disassembled and said, "Well, maybe. You see, I don't like all those dark ugly pieces." Mama said, "What did you do with them?" I got down off my chair and went into the living room, with Mama following me. I picked up a cushion and dropped it on the floor—and another one—and there where I'd put them were the pieces. I was surprised at how many of them there were! Mama laughed again, "Oh Rachel Naomi." And she gathered them all up in her apron, and we went back to the puzzle thing. She dumped them out onto the table, and her hands started moving fast—putting pieces in, along the straight sides and connected along a line— with the pieces that had dark red, some gold, dark blues, and suddenly she was making a picture—just like the one on the box! There was a thin line—it was the sun when it just starts to come up stretched out along the beach. The sand was dark and shadowed, and the sky was night with just a little bit of it going gray and silver. My eyes must have been like great big plates, "How did you do that, Mama?"

"It was easy, honey. I'd been working on it for so long that I knew what was missing, and we needed all those dark pieces. I knew exactly where they should go; I just didn't know where they had got to. Isn't it lovely?" My head was going up and down and I was thinking, when can we go to the beach again and watch the sun come out of the night and run across the water and the sand. But Mama was looking at me "funny" again, and she said, "Rachel, you didn't like the dark pieces and called them ugly. But you have to learn that the night and darkness and even what we call ugly is part of life and necessary. We can't see the light or appreciate it unless there is darkness too. See how beautiful the darkness is when you look at it with the light?" I nodded, and she went on, "and you can't go and hide it somewhere— like under the cushions in the sofa. You have to put it in its right place so that it and the light can be together.

Rachel, now in her sixties, says that she knew that truth when she was young—that you can't hide the darkness or ignore it or try to get rid of it, in the sofa cushions or anywhere else—but as she grew, she forgot and had to spend many years remembering that wisdom her Mama told her and to integrate it into her own life—her operations, her disease, those whom she sought to help as they tried to heal or continued to suffer and die, or those whom she comforted as they were with those they loved as they died. Like Rachel as a child and as a grown woman, we must learn to love the darkness and see it as essential if we are ever to know and appreciate light— whether it is the light of day, or the lights of night: moon and stars and planets; or the light of what we call insight, wisdom, understanding, meaning, and truth. We are invited to know and love dark wisdom, dark in the daylight, dark dreams, dark knowing, deep dark meaning, and dark truth as intimately and truly as its soul sister or brother the light. (In many cultures, the moon is a man, in others a woman, and the same for the sun—it is described and spoken about as either, or both.)

There are so many words that contradict this understanding of inclusion, diversity, plurality, and balance in our traditions, spiritual writings, and even in our liturgical calendar, especially in the Northern Hemisphere and the West—where Light/Easter and Resurrection are celebrated in spring, ignoring that in the other half of the world, it comes in the midst of the world going dark, as the seasons are in their opposite in the Southern Hemisphere. There is the season of Advent—a time of darkness, silence, waiting for the mystery of incarnation—God born with us as a human child, leaping down from heaven in the dark of the night, mysterious, hidden, and unknown, but it is short—often only three weeks, and most of the emphasis is on the light shattering the darkness. This is all well and good, but there is need for more emphasis on the nine months where the child lived in darkness and secrecy, slowly becoming more human, even "growing in wisdom, age/time and grace" until it was time for him to be born. There is the unknown time of almost thirty years when Jesus lives daily and nightly in the turning of light and dark, beginning each day as a Jew as dusk and darkness begin at sundown, with the first twelve hours of day, and especially Sabbath as night and darkness, followed by the morning that comes forth out of the night.

Paul writes these words in the first of his letters to the community at Thessalonica:

> But you, brothers [sisters or beloved of God], are not in darkness, for that day to overtake you like a thief. For all of you are children of the light and children of the day. We are not of the night or of darkness. Therefore, let us not sleep as the rest do, but let us stay alert and sober. Those who sleep go to sleep at night, and those who are drunk get drunk at night. But since we are of the day, let us be sober, putting on the breastplate of faith and love and the helmet that is the hope of salvation. For God did not destine us for wrath, but to gain salvation through our Lord Jesus Christ, who died for us, so that whether we are awake or asleep we may live together with him. Therefore, encourage one another and build one another up, as indeed you do. (1 Thess 5:4–11)

Like the militaristic imagery of battle and protection, the strident exclusivity of the negative aspects of night, darkness, the connection to thievery, drunkenness, even sleep, and being only children of the light and the day must be reconfigured and made to include the reality that all is holy, all is one, all is revelatory, all is to be honored, not just one side of a simplistic image or equation. We are as much the children of the night, children of darkness, children of mystery, children of what is unknown, and children of the universe made of light and dark. It is only the very last line where the completeness and the "other side" is mentioned: "Whether we are awake or asleep we live together in him" (v. 10). We must read and listen to our traditions and amend them, extend them, and remake them in the wisdom of the Creator's words after each day expressed "and God saw that it was good." All is good, every day.[3]

Now, for us, who are creatures of the day and the night, of light and darkness, what can this mean for our living, our lifestyles, our prayer, and our sense of who we are and how we relate to others, to the world, and to God? There is a story from the monastic tradition of Theophane that is enlightening and thought-provoking that can perhaps get us moving in new directions of including what might appear to be contradictory or opposite realities together. I heard it a long time ago from a monk, aptly named Theophane.

Once upon a time, there was a monk. He'd been one for a while, but he was always wondering, what exactly is a monk? He obeyed the rules, said his prayers, lived with his community, even had the full habit, but did what he do make him a monk? One day, a visiting monk was giving some talks as part of their yearly retreat, and he decided to ask him, "What is a monk?" The other monk's reaction startled him—it was another question. "Do you mean in the daytime or at night?" He had no idea what the man was talking about. The monk was silent. He didn't know where to go or what to say next.

The other said simply, "A monk, like everyone else, is

a creature of contraction and expansion. During the day, we are contracted—bound and enclosed by walls, our place in this world, even our habit and habits, our rule of when and how to pray, our meals, and we mostly do what everyone expects a monk to do. But at night—ah, we expand. Nothing can contain us, no walls, no habit, no rules, no traditions, not even anyone else. At night, in the dark and the depths, there is no limit, we move through the whole world, through the night, touching even the moon and the stars and outer darkness of the universe."

The questioning monk didn't know what to say or to think. His mind went to philosophy, theology, even poetry, and he started to react, saying, "Oh, you're talking about our real body that we inhabit during the day...and..." but he got no further. The other responded, saying, "That is one way to think about who we are as human beings, but it's not necessarily helpful. We are one, body (flesh and blood and bone) and soul, mind, spirit, heart (will). We are even one with everyone else, all the beloved of our God who is One. During the day, we live breathing in, contracting if you will, relating and being in contact with those around us, but at night, we live, breathing out, expanding out to touch others, reaching even to the stars and beyond. We are meant to be measured, if you will, by how many and how deeply we know and touch others in God." The monk just stood there, and the other smiled and walked away. Then he turned and said, "I so love the night!"

The man who told me the story added on the last line. I had shared with him a poem and that was the opening line. He laughed and I did too—we both have so loved the night. But what if this is true? What if we are to measure a Christian, one who believes in God, by who they touch at night, at how much they have learned of what it means to be human and to expand to reach out and touch others, even to the number of the stars? What if?

Just this past year, I discovered something shocking and yet comforting that has led me to many insights and understanding. It was right before Advent and I was looking for stories and images to go along with the Scripture readings. It was the year of Matthew, which is a Gospel of angels and dreams and stars, which all can mean different aspects of the one thing—revelation and annunciations of God. I read in a piece by Madeleine L'Engle that the word *disaster* means *dis-*, "separation" and *-aster*, "star." It tries to say that a disaster tells us that we are separated from the stars! The stars give us a place to stand, to be, and at the same time, give us direction, a sense of where we are, and therefore, where we can go on this earth and at sea. An English friend added that I was correct, that there are places in England that begin with and use this syllable *dis-* to speak of isolation, misery, and disorientation, separation from others. My Nana used to tell me often "that only those who walk in darkness ever see the stars." I assumed for years it was her wisdom, but I'm sure that is collective wisdom that all Nanas and many of our elders know. The night is essential for seeing stars and the moon and inserting ourselves into the larger universe and sense of our place in the world. The world of sky, night, the luminaries of moon, stars, and other bodies in the darkness are said by many to be the first book of revelation that God ever wrote, and so "the heavens reveal the glory of God" for those who can see, read, and even hear the singing of the stars and the depth and vastness of the deep emptiness of their silence. We get our bearings and steer home by the stars—so that if we know that language of the night and sky, we are never really lost or "at sea."

The Jewish community and tradition reveals that God, blessed be his name, hid the original light of "let there be Light" in the darkness, the endless mystery and depths of the Torah. The Word of God is that other source for getting our bearings and directions to steer by, knowing who we are and who God is, as well as revealing to us the mystery that encompasses both the light and the darkness, the word/sound/silence that both reveals and conceals God.

One of the most oft-repeated refrains in the Gospels is the reference to Jesus, who also "loves the night" and slips away as often as he can when night falls and darkness comes to pray and to be alone with God. It is his source of power, strength, and sense of identity, where he refuels, is resourced, and is resounded by the dark presence and absence. It is where he goes to find God and comes to know God as Spirit and as the one who fathers him and gives birth to him. Each night is a womb to be immersed in, where his body and soul, his spirit and will are graced—renewed—and where he expands and stretches out, becoming ever more human, more holy, more one with God and with everyone summoned forth from the dark, the waters, and the wind with the words "Let there be light." For that to occur, there must first be the words and the command "Let there be night." The Gospels seek to tell us who Jesus was/is, but most of the telling takes place in the daylight. What was Jesus like in the night, in the hidden darkness within and without?

We read and hear, "Rising very early before dawn, he left and went off to a deserted place, where he prayed" (Mark 1:35).[4] This sets the pattern for the entire Gospel. At the end, we will read, "Very early in the morning, on the first day of the week, just before dawn" (Mark 16:2). This has been the traditional rendering of the first words of the account of the resurrection of Jesus. A recent translation makes it even clearer: "Extremely early on the first of the Sabbaths they came to the tomb. The sun had already risen" (Mark 16:2). As with the mystery of the Incarnation, God becoming flesh, becoming human, the mystery of the resurrection, God raising his beloved child Jesus from the dead in the power of the Spirit is presented as happening in the darkest part of the night before dawn. It is the dark and night that gives birth to new life, to the Light that is a person now, to hope, and to resurrection. The mystery is unseen, with no witnesses, hidden in just another night that is so "good."

There is so much more to say of the dark, of the night, of the unknown and its power, its place of sourcing and birthing, its depth and its mystery that both repels us and draws us into its embrace. All the hours, including of course, the hours of the night, are rife and dense with wisdom, knowledge, and the presence of God.

Someone once said that poetry is born of darkness; perhaps it is best to end by introducing two of my favorite poems to you as a nudge into our own darkness and night when it comes—tonight. In his poem, "East

Coker," T. S. Eliot writes that "the darkness shall be the light, and the stillness the dancing." The other is Denise Levertov's "Writing in the Dark," which someone wrote out for me in calligraphy, in two versions. One is white ink against a black night of a page and the other is black ink against a white background. It came with a note that this was penned in both ways to imitate the Torah, which is often described as "Black Fire on White Fire." I treasure its startling different revelations about the power of words and its instruction to "Keep writing in the dark."

REFLECTIONS AND PRACTICES

1. Would you describe yourself as being afraid of the dark—and if so, what is it that you fear? What of night and darkness draws you and suggests there might be something there?

2. Try taking a walk in the dark. It is said that our eyes actually see better in the dark, once they acclimate, and our hearing is more acute. Walk or sit in the dark and listen. Then let the dark outside you merge with the dark silence within. What is it like for you to be in the dark? Is praying different in the dark?

3. There is an ancient Gaelic prayer:

   As the rain hides the stars and the clouds veil the blue skies,
   so the dark happenings of my life hide the shining of your face.

Yet, if I may hold your hand in the darkness, it is enough.
Since I know that, though I may stumble in my going, you do not fall. Amen.

Have you ever had the experience of the dark being comforting, peaceful, filled with mystery and awe? Have you ever blessed the darkness of night or the darkness within you? What would that kind of blessing prayer be like?

9

LISTENING TO
YOUR BODY

*I find ecstasy in living. The mere sense of
living is joy enough.*

—Emily Dickinson

*We are travelling with tremendous speed
toward a star in the Milky Way. A great
repose is visible on the face of the Earth.
My heart's a little fast. Otherwise,
everything's fine.*

—Bertolt Brecht

How do we listen to our own bodies? We are made of
flesh and blood and bone, heart, entrails, skin, and much
that is tangible. Yet we are made of soul and spirit, emotion, memories, five (or some believe six) senses, and less
tangible but just as powerful elements. What makes up a
human being? Some say humans are made of stories—or

songs—or just what can be reduced to basic elements in a Petri dish—the bulk of us being just water and a few minerals. We know a great deal about the human body, but it doesn't always factor into our conception of ourselves. Sadly, it often doesn't help us to appreciate what an amazing thing a human body is. Just a few things should stagger our awareness:

> 100,000 heartbeats per day
> 100,000 miles of blood vessels in the human body
> 100 million light-sensitive cells in the retina of eyes
> 4,000–10,000 smells can be distinguished

We should stand in awe of what we are just physically! We usually take human bodies for granted, including our own, until something happens.

This chapter will begin with a Jewish story from the tradition of the Baal Shem Tov. The story is about our bodies and souls, what makes us holy, and the power of touch and the presence of a human body, one upon another. I hope it will introduce many of the insights and concepts that we will touch upon in this chapter on listening to the human body—and on listening to our own bodies.

Once upon a time, the Baal Shem Tov was teaching his many disciples the essence and importance of sleep as part of the discipline of being human and holy, but also as a time when God works on us unbeknownst to us. He reminded them that when we sleep and rest, God borrows our souls for that time and takes us to heaven and then returns them to us, renewed and refreshed when we awake in the morning. Though he insisted that they take his words to heart, there was one person in the world at that time who never really slept or rested completely—and it was the Baal Shem Tov himself! Oh, he went to sleep at night, and God took his soul to heaven, but he refused to rest. Even while he slept, he pushed his soul to move upward through the heavens. He didn't just want to rest so close to the Divine while he slept at night, he wanted to be reunited with God, and so before he slept, he pushed his soul to keep reaching for God even while he slept. With each passing night, he got closer and closer to actually uniting with God.

Now, it is believed that right in front of God's throne there is a curtain made of woven light. On the curtain are imprinted images from everything on earth, all that is created and all that has transpired in history— happening at that moment and what is to come. The curtain is the last thing that stands between someone and the presence of The Holy. The curtain moves, like water, like silk rippling in the air, like a breath of perfume. When God looks at and through the curtain, God views all that is on the other side—the past, the present, and the future—all at once.

Well, finally, after years of seeking to get close enough to God, to reach past that curtain and see God face-to-face, and even reach out and touch God, the restless driving soul of the Baal Shem Tov got as close as anyone has ever been. Even though he was asleep in his bed at home, he knew he was that close—at that final curtain. He knew from his study and belief that if he just strained one more night, this night, he could pass through the curtain. He wouldn't die, but he would be released, freed forever from the constraints of this world, of earth and his mortal body. He would no longer have to struggle with physical weakness, his mind wandering, lack of zeal in his work and prayer, all the struggles that being in his body in the world entail. He would be holy! He'd be perfect! He'd attain, while still on earth, what so many others must wait to know and experience after life ends here. While still on earth, going about his daily duties and living, he would be united, at one with God! He was so close to his dream coming true—he thought of all he could teach his disciples and share with those who faltered and stumbled. And he reached for the curtain shimmering right before him.

Just at that moment as his hand moved out to go through the curtain, down on earth where his body slept, his wife, who lay beside him in their bed, moved. She stirred and instinctively turned toward him, and her hand reached for his face and she gently, tenderly brushed his cheek and sighed. The Baal Shem Tov shuddered and was thrown off his intent. He pulled his hand back with a jerk! For his soul realized in that moment when she touched him, her body warming his body, that holiness, that perfection, that becoming what God has dreamed us to be at our beginnings is not in some heaven to be strained after day and night, but we become whole, body and soul and spirit, right here on earth. His soul dropped down into his body on the bed, and he whispered a prayer of thanks to the Holy One for

restoring his soul and leaned into his wife's body, blessing God for her, for it was she that God used to reach
him before it was too late—she protected him and with a
touch of her hand on his face, restored him.

It's a remarkable story, gathering together many
elements of what it means to be a human being, to be
religious and want to be holy/wholly/whole and the
depth of the connection between our bodies and souls
and to one another. For now, I will not comment on the
story, but keep it in mind and heart as you read the
chapter.

> *The world is not to be put in order; the world*
> *is order, incarnate. It is for us to harmonize*
> *with this order.*
>
> —Henry Miller

Many people we call artists try to remind us and
share with us what they are drawn by and driven to try
to express, even just to create descriptions of, or to repli-
cate in some form in stone, cloth, paint, words, metal,
clay, and even discarded materials, what they see and
sense of who we are. This is what Auguste Rodin, sculp-
tor, said about the human body:

> Beauty is character and expression. Now, there
> is nothing in nature that has more character
> than the human body. It evokes through its
> strength or its grace the most varied images.
> At one moment, it resembles a flower; the
> bending of torso imitates the stem, while the

smile of the breast, head and gleaming hair corresponds to the blooming of the corolla. At another moment, it recalls a supple liana, a shrub with a fine and daring camber....At another time the body curved back is like a spring, like a beautiful bow from which Eros aims his invisible arrows. Another time, it is an urn. I have often had a model sit on the floor and turn her back to me with her legs and arms drawn before her. In this position only the silhouette of the back, which narrows at the waist and widens at the hip, appears, and this forms a vase with an exquisite contour: the amphora that holds the life of the future in its flanks.[1]

There are as many ways to speak about the human body as there are human beings in the world! But what is it like to be inside, to dwell and abide in one's body? This body we inhabit is our first and most intimate home. Again, there are those who specialize in speaking about being a human being and being in a body. Philosophers, theologians, spiritual directors, counselors, psychologists, physicians, religious preachers—the litany is endless. They all speak from their discipline and perspectives, explaining, exposing, and even demanding how to live in one's body. They range from condemnation to soaring mysticism in seeking to reveal what it means to experience the range of life in one's own body. Here is a contemporary expression from Thomas Merton, a Trappist monk who wrote many books about the connective tissues of body and soul, both on theoretical levels and more personally in his diaries and poems.

> There is in all visible things an invisible fecundity, a dimmed light, a meek namelessness, a hidden wholeness. This mysterious unity and integrity is wisdom, the mother of all. There is in all things an inexhaustible sweetness and purity, a silence that is a font of action and joy. It rises up in wordless gentleness and flows out to me from the unseen roots of all created being. This is at once my own being, my own nature, and the Gift of my Creator's Thought and Art with me, speaking as Hagia Sophia, sent to me from the depths of divine fecundity.[2]

So much of what is written about being human, about living in a body, seems devoid of the physical, of the flesh whether it is the daily movement and functions of the body or the extremes of suffering, being born and dying, sexuality, making love, and making new human bodies and the whole symphony and cacophony of sensations that abide in us all. Some poets and mystics do express desires, yearnings, lusts, yens, attractions, resistances, physical sensations, and bodily needs and are often censored and pilloried for their work. Walt Whitman's work *Leaves of Grass* was shocking to many, and he first had to have it privately published. It is said that these lines were some of the poet's own favorites.

I sing the body electric,
The armies of those I love engirth me and I
    engirth them,
They will not let me off till I go with them,
    respond to them,
And discorrupt them, and charge them full with
    the charge of the soul.[3]

All too often, especially in Western culture and religions, Christianity and Judaism included, there has been
a disconnect about being human and living in a body.
In fact, it is more often described as "having a body"
rather than living in one or dwelling in one. As developed from Greek philosophy, Christianity teaches that
we are made up of body and soul. We begin with separation and disunity and dislocation. There is the notion
of spirit as well—a triad of body, soul, and spirit. Even
growing up, there was the oft-repeated phrase, simplistic, demanding, and descriptive—"If it feels good, it's bad
for you, and if it hurts, it's good for you." Maxims like
this were a dime a dozen and taken very seriously. Even
famous and well-loved saints that we were to model and
imitate like Francis of Assisi, who loved all creatures
and the creation, treated his own body horrendously,
referring to it as "Brother Ass"—though at the end of his
life, lying on the ground naked, it is said that he asked
forgiveness of his own body for the way he had treated
it and neglected to honor it.

The interpretation of creation stories from Genesis
and traditions of belief, as well as the dichotomy (inherent in much of Greek thought) between what is holy and

unholy or what is sacred and what is profane, what is good and what is evil, leached into the perceived and taught parts of us in opposition—body and soul. Body was the one to be contained, disciplined, beaten into submission, denied, even ignored so that the soul could rule and gain the upper hand. It was taught that our souls were trapped in our bodies and would not be released or set free until death. We lived with a war going on inside us perpetually and it is still alive and well in most of us, with remnants and whole areas of our lives that have been bent, twisted, condemned, or seen as less than holy or even desirable.

Once, when I was trying to write a poem for a high school class—it was supposed to be on a theme that blended and spoke about what it meant to have both a body and a soul—I wrote something that I sensed was very important but also knew immediately that it was definitely at odds with what I was supposed to be proclaiming poetically. What if our bodies dwelled in our souls (the very opposite of what was assumed) and our souls sought expression through our bodies? It was the beginning of the sense that we are integrated, intimate, and whole as created and that rather than a war being waged within us, perhaps what we were experiencing was the natural processes of growth, development, and choices of becoming what was born of these foundational elements continuing the process of creation.

Someone once said that the Spirit (meaning God) needed flesh to work on earth and used our flesh to continue to express the Divine on earth. St. Teresa of Avila, a very pragmatic yet mystical lady, wrote as part of a prayer,

> Christ has no body now but yours,
> No hands, no feet on earth but yours,
> Yours are the eyes through which he looks
>   with compassion on this world.

It is a remarkable explanation of our bodies as necessary for any life on earth beyond being a body that has physical characteristics.

Someone once said that if you change the stories, you can change realities. I was not alone in my questionings and wonderings, and this underlying sense and thought nagged at me as a constant background in all I read, heard, and was taught. Another piece of the puzzle was a description of the human body that I heard while studying Hebrew/Aramaic and the background of being Jewish at the time of Jesus. It is also a way of describing how human beings perceive themselves now, in an ancient tradition of many Native peoples and in most of Asia. It is looking at the human body as a map where you can find various ways of being human and expressing what you know, think, feel, sense, and remember. It is a fascinating representation that roots us more in our bodies than many more philosophical or theological explanations might.

A series of questions begins to draw the map of the human body. Where do you keep or store your feelings? This first question brings a range of answers: heart, skin, muscles, stomach, or depending on what feelings they are, they are kept in various places in the body—more painful ones in back or neck muscles; more pleasant ones in the heart; some people even say many feelings are kept in the sense of taste. For those who originated the map, feelings are kept in your lower abdomen and stomach.

The next question: Where do you keep your memories? Again a raft of answers: in my head, my brain, my muscles (many therapies teach that memories are stored in muscles/at junctures where the body moves—knees, elbows, ankles, spine, and neck and that these memories can cause muscles to cramp, shorten, and tighten around these joints). The answer: in your lower abdomen and guts! For the rest of the questions, the question will be asked and you can answer them for yourself and the answer will be provided.

Next question: What do you keep in your head? That is the place of doubts and questions. What is kept in your throat? Your soul is in your throat! Where is your spirit? Your spirit is in your breath and breathing. What is kept in your feet? This answer, which is obvious for some but not for others, is where what connects you to the earth, what grounds you is kept. What do you store in your skin? Feelings, touch, power to heal, comfort as well as to inflict pain. What do you keep in your heart? This is the question and the answer that most people in the West find the most difficult to answer and find the response the hardest to accept because it has such drastic consequences. The heart is where our will dwells. So, such a simple and powerful commandment and statement as "You shall love the Lord your God with all your heart" and "You shall love your neighbor with all your heart" is radically altered. Most of Western humans tend to think of the heart being connected to feelings and emotions, likes/dislikes, loves and hates, rather than intent, choice, and the will to do what is true, most human and like God.

This map situates more theoretical concepts of soul, spirit, personality, and what constitutes much of human living solidly in our bodies. It is not based, of course, on modern medicine or concepts of physics, but it can provide an opening into looking and listening to our bodies so that we can begin to appreciate what it means to live in one's body and attend to it as you can attend to another person's voice, appearance, mien, gestures, posture, touch, nearness or distance, eyes, smell, and so forth.

As odd as it may sound, it must be stated clearly: Our bodies matter; matter matters. Our bodies matter to each of us. Our bodies matter to others and our bodies matter to God! Everyone's body matters to God, and we must begin to look at our own and others' bodies as mattering to God—and that they are all "very good." The mystery of the incarnation that is a cornerstone for all other beliefs in Christianity states amazingly and earth-shatteringly that God—the Divine—became a human being with flesh, blood, bone, and every organ we have and dwells among us still. God did not just take the appearance of being a human being, or become partly human and remain the other part Divine. God, in the person, the flesh of Jesus, became a human being with a body, the breath of life that began and stopped, and a soul. Jesus born, growing, living, being sick, suffering, rejoicing, and delighting in all that being flesh and blood entails and engenders and all its range of feeling and sensation, along with awareness, limitedness, and mortality that brought him to his dying, he shared and knew in himself, as we know in our bodies, our lives, and our souls. This mystery, this reality changes everything about what it means to be a human being, what life is for and how to live for all human beings. Jesus' words attest to this opening in the limitless possibilities of how we are to live when he says, "I have come that you might have life and have it evermore abundantly" (John 10:10). This statement is parsed in the plural—it is life ever more abundantly for all human beings, not just a few or those who believe in them, but for all.

One of the stories of our beginnings from the Book of Genesis: the first story we are told, in words more than six thousand years old, is that we "are made in the image and likeness of God" by God to abide in creation and be in relation to creation, as God is in relation to us—preserving and being careful of all of it, so that what is innate in all that is made may continue to develop and evolve for future generations. It is deceptively simple and profound, and it demands that we obey what is innate in us—to reflect the image and likeness of the Holy, the Divine, in our bodies and lives.

> And God said, "Let us make man in our image, after our likeness. They shall rule the fish of the seas, the birds of the sky, the cattle, the whole earth, and all the creeping things that creep on earth. And God created man in His

image, in the image of God He created him; male and female He created them. God blessed them....And it was so. And God saw all that He had made, and found it very good. And there was evening and there was morning, the sixth day. (Gen 1:26–31)

There are innumerable commentaries, midrash, and traditions on the meaning of practically every phrase and word in the story, but there are a few very clear agreements. All human beings are "very good." All human beings, male and female, were created together, simultaneously, and this difference or plurality is part of the essence of the one image and likeness of God—every human being singularly speaks a Word of God. The *adam* or the human is more truly translated as "the earthling," as we are made of the stuff of earth, sky, waters, and all that has come before us in the story. We live with one another and with all the other creatures of the earth on the earth. This relationship is bound up with responsibility for and with all else that has been made. We have been blessed to continue creation—both in bringing forth other human beings and to care for and preserve all these creatures, the earth, seas, and air, acting as stewards of the One who created all. The beginning stories are trying to express who we are and what we might become. From this initial emerging forth on the earth, the creation process proceeds and is to continue to both reveal the interrelatedness of all, including God, and the reality that creation will not cease to evolve and grow, to expand and be available to sustain itself and everything for the future. We are blessed along with everything else and entrusted with this shared likeness of God. Again—once we are part of the equation—it is all very good.

Where does that leave us—body, soul, and spirit? Our bodies have breath, the essence of life that we call spirit. Our soul is our principle of existence—not just as a living being in a body, but it can describe our singular sense of existence—personality, sense of identity, personhood, the meaning of who we are as an individual human being, like no other, but saying something no one else does about God. Our bodies are critical to existence in this world and time. All three are interwoven in us like a braid. Nothing is trapped inside of or imprisoning anything else—all moves together as part of being a living human being. If one does not have breath/spirit, then we are physically dead, and when that occurs, the body disintegrates without its sustaining breath/spirit. It is believed that the soul that is the singular seed or essence of the human person dwells in the human being as spirited flesh, and that its existence can and does continue in some form when the body dies and the breath stops. In the Genesis story, this is one of the meanings of the first words of the Creator: "Let there be light"—that in that moment the souls of all humans that would ever be were summoned forth from God and are held in God until our time of righteousness, justice, and holiness in time, upon the earth.

All of this assumes a belief in God who creates and sustains and is in some sort of distinct relationship to all life and to each individual form of life, including human beings that constitute a conscious likeness to God.

The Jewish tradition has its way of speaking about what constitutes being human. Simply expressed, it is believed that the human soul is composed of three parts: The lowest or basest part is called *nefesh*, which literally translates as "animation." This animation or force of life is shared with all creation: birds, animals, plants, and so on. The second part is *ruah*, which is "spirit" or often translated now as "personality," and this is shared with animals. The third part is *neshamah*, which is "breath." This is the understanding of Genesis 2:7 when God breathed the *nishmat chayim*, "the breath of God" into Adam (the earthling). This *neshamah* is what separates human beings from the rest of creation because it was given directly by God to human beings. There are many ways to speak about this *neshamah* because it is seen as the portion of the human person that is attuned more directly to the Divine (this does not mean the other parts aren't attuned). In Proverbs, it is written, "The *neshamah* of a person is the lamp of God, searching all the inward parts" (20:27).

All this is prologue to listening to our bodies as a practice and way of being in the world. Our bodies are the place that we inhabit and how we are present to the world and others. Information, data, and life come into us from our senses, through our skin, our minds, our experiences, and our very presence. This begins with being here now. I almost called this chapter "Being Hear Now," playing on the words *here/hear*, expressing the idea of being in the moment, becoming aware of where we are physically and what is physically around us. We breathe air, whether it is fresh, full of smells and odors, rancid with pollutants, carrying rain, cold, warmth, winds—every sort of weather and particles from around the globe. We take it in and purify it and exhale to live another moment. We feel, sensing those same weathers, and the skin and bones, flesh of other humans, dogs/cats, pets, the bark of trees, coarseness of wood, textures—in work, in art, in the clothing we wear, and what we use for shelter and adornment. We touch what soothes, calms, pleasures, elicits pain; shedding tears, sweat, odors that attract and repel, and secretions that move us to arousal, elation, sexual and physical union, exhaustion and a sense of being poured out, lost, united, in communion or isolated—the litany is as long as a lifetime of moments of experience: moments to be repeated or shunned and shrunk from knowing yet again.

We are surrounded by sound and draw it in and seek to filter it, disappear into it, get lost in it, create it, drown it out, relate to it—in the human voice and all manner of technology, machinery in transportation, communication, work, production, and destruction. On occasion, others "listen" to our bodies: through heartbeats, rhythms, pulses; by observing brain scans; through lungs functioning, breathing, rasping; through our throats and what is caught in them, causing us to gasp, gag, lose our voices, cough, sing, croak, and whisper. We can sit, gathering our body, mind, and spirit together and concentrate on our breath, watch our breathing, count breaths, slowing down our respiratory systems and stilling the pace of our heartbeat, while emptying our minds and receding from outside sound.

We can, in a way, disappear inside our bodies. At the other extreme, we can push our heartbeat and the pace of our legs, our lungs, and breathing in exercise, in sport, and competition–whether against or relative to others or our "own personal best"–straining against usual norms and ways of being and moving. We check our pulse and heart rate to make sure we're getting the benefit of whatever we are doing, releasing endorphins, accelerating our metabolisms to burn energy, fat, and turn calories into more constructive nutrients for our bodies to use to keep us fit. So we sweat, blush, get hot flashes, feel our hearts skipping beats, wavering, breaking rhythms, and feel our bodies reacting in every cell to what "is off."

We taste. We eat. We drink. We swallow and start the processes of digesting, metabolizing, turning food into our bodies, and expelling what needs to go. We taste our own sweat, sometimes our own tears, the sweat of others, and more rarely the tears of another. We taste (and smell) the ozone in the air, the salt in the air, metallic substances. We have favorite tastes that we indulge in over and over again or try to limit and tastes that repulse us, those we avoid at all costs. We suck on our own skin when we burn ourselves or try to extract a splinter. We taste the skin and flesh of those we love, giving pleasure, drawing as close to another human being as we can–merging flesh. We know the taste of blood–a sliced finger, a bloody nose, biting down on our tongues, or splitting a lip. We bleed from our internal organs as a sign of something that is wrong with us. At least half the human race bleeds regularly in rhythms with the larger world of moon and tides and time, bound to the ability to continue the human race and give birth to our own.

All our senses are interrelated, separate, and distinct, and yet interactive with the others. We see and our eyes are connected to our ears. Our sense of smell can be extremely strong and evocative. Smells evoke memories and places and experiences that we are often unaware of or have forgotten, even deliberately ignored, and a smell, however faint, can bring it all back to our present consciousness, where it must be dealt with. We associate smell with certain people, places, and the conditions of people—disease, long periods of time without water. They can be positive as with perfume, elixirs, and scents we wear, or repellent as being jammed in a crowded space in the heat or with unwashed bodies. There are people who say they can even smell when someone is angry or about to do something violent. It is believed by many people that our hearing sense is the last one to leave when we are dying, so people draw close, speaking, singing, whispering to help someone die.

All of our senses both draw in and seek to express the outside world, other people, and what is within us. We are a maze, a web, and an intricate weave of amazing "stuff" that is our bodies. We dwell in this space, move, live, and have our being for years, decades—our lifetime that we measure in feet and inches, height and width and weight.

But do we listen to our bodies, let alone appreciate them? Abraham Heschel once said, "We teach the children how to measure and how to weigh. We fail to teach them how to revere, how to sense wonder and awe."[4] To extend this reality—the Irish poet W. B. Yeats wrote, "The world is full of magic things, patiently waiting on our senses to grow sharper." Not only is the world full of magic things, but also our own bodies, minds, and souls—as are the bodies, minds, and souls of all other human beings.

Our religious traditions, teachings, practices, and attitudes toward our bodies have not often been positive over the last thousands of years. This is a general observation, it is true, and sadly a reality for many people. This is especially expressed in regard to our bodies and our sexuality. Our sexuality is often seen as something to be controlled, disciplined, ignored, chastised, belittled, shamed, a source of embarrassment, and something that is best not expressed, except in proscribed functions. It has been taught that to be celibate, to remain a virgin, is a higher form of living than to marry or remain single. The list of saints in the Church is an overwhelming testament to this belief and encouragement, though more than 97 percent of the human race does not follow this exhortation.

We so often do not honor and incorporate the effects and grace that are embedded in us by the goodness of our Creator God let alone the grace, holiness, and awe that is seeded and always in our bodies by the mystery of the incarnation. God is embodied in the body of Jesus. God is embodied in our bodies. We all express a unique revelation of God in our bodies and souls. It is in and through our sexuality that each of us expresses what it means to love bodily with others. Pragmatically, sexuality is about keeping the human race in existence (there really isn't any problem with that reality, as there are over seven billion people on the earth at the moment.) There is a joke often told in classes on sexuality that the commandment to "Be fruitful and multiply" is really the only one that most people do—often without even thinking much about it!

There is an intimate connection between sexuality and the act of procreation—the seeding and bearing of a child into existence. Yet for human beings, what if this connection in sexuality isn't the primary way that human beings live in the world, with others and with God? We are so much more than our bodily functions—including having sexual intercourse and having children as a possible result. If sexuality is the way a person uniquely expresses their image of God and how God loves through them, then we are sexual beings throughout our lives and with a range of expression. What if our sexuality is how God loves other human beings using our bodies? How do we, who are created by God, dwell in God, and beloved of God, love others in and with our own bodies?

It has to be expressed through all our senses, our actions, choices, words, silence, work, touch, ways of sharing life with another, many others, and showing our appreciation for the goodness of all creation and all peoples. We are always sexual in this sense. We are sexual whether we are married, not married, never married, widowed, and in every vocation or way of life. We are male and female, human beings created for more than making sure the human race doesn't die out. Women were created to be more than those who receive a man's sperm in order to give birth, just as men were created to be more than those who seed sperm in a woman's womb. The question of why we live, of why we have been created, and what constitutes being a human being is the more important, more fundamental question and the more insistent and demanding question. Simply put, what is the meaning of being a human being in a body of spirit and soul?

And it matters not whether we are male or female! We are human first and foremost, each and all of us. I once heard a sermon from Rabbi Regina Sara Jonas in which she said, "God planted in our hearts skills and a vocation without asking about gender." The words registered like a thunderbolt and have echoed clearly ever since inside me—they entered my ears and shot straight through to my brain, my heart, and my whole body reverberated. They are true and they apply to everything about us. We are holy in our bodies, our flesh, our spirit, as well as what we do with our minds, or words, or the way we make our living and our way in the world. We are not at odds with parts of ourselves. We are not disordered. We are not separated into body and soul. Parts of our body are not better than other parts, each and all are essential and we are whole together.

How do we talk about listening to our bodies if it is not connected to how we listen to the bodies of other human beings? It is here—in our flesh and spirit—where we perhaps can find our soul in listening to the in-spirited bodies and souls of other human beings. Karl Menninger, founder of the Menninger Clinic in Topeka, Kansas, in 1893, said this: "The central purpose of each life should be to dilute the misery of the world."

Martin Luther King Jr. said it this way: "An individual has not started living until he or she can rise above the narrow confines of his or her individualistic concerns to the broader concerns of all humanity." In one of his speeches, he tried to make this mutual and universal connection very practical, based in what we do with our bodies daily.

> When we get up in the morning, we go into the bathroom where we reach for a sponge provided for us by a Pacific Islander....We reach for soap created by a Frenchman. [Then at breakfast we] drink coffee provided by a South American, or tea by a Chinese, or cocoa by a West African....And before [we've] finished breakfast, [we've] depended on more than half the world.[5]

Another way of saying something of this reality, which might seem more poetic given its image, is really just as pragmatic. Brother David Steindl-Rast has said, "Each string of a wind harp responds with a different note to the same breeze. What activity makes you personally resonate most strongly, most deeply, with the wind of the Spirit that blows where it wills?"[6] The Holy One made so many different kinds of people, why would there be only one or two ways to be holy or to express our image and likeness of God in our bodies and lives?

(To borrow from Martin Buber, "God made so many different kinds of people; why would God allow only one way to worship?")

The story of the transfiguration of Jesus, who takes three of his disciples up a mountain to pray, tells us much about being human. After Jesus is *transfigured*—the prefix *trans-* is a preposition in Latin meaning "to cross over," "pass through," "see and hear through" (like the curtain in the opening story), and the word *figure*, meaning "the human body" as in the artistic discipline of drawing the human figure—the transfiguration shows forth Jesus—body, soul, and spirit—to the disciples. The disciples, especially Peter, react to what has happened by saying how good it is to be there, to have seen and experienced Jesus through and through. They want to stay on the mountain, build tents so that they can dwell there, and not have to go down the mountain again. They have caught a glimpse of the glory of God shining through the body of Jesus, and they want to stay in that moment and not let it go—ever (see Matt 17:1-8).

But Jesus does not even respond to Peter's suggestion. Instead, he leads them down the mountain and is immediately met by human misery, human beings coping with disease and need, specifically a father distraught about his young child who suffers from epilepsy. He pleads with Jesus to help his child, who has seizures, who often falls into fire or water. The disciples couldn't do anything for him (see Matt 17:14-16). Peter, and most of us, most of the time, would prefer to stay on the mountain and draw out the moment of ecstasy as long as possible and altogether avoid the misery and daily mess that also makes up our lives. Body and soul and spirit—we all live with both extremes and ordinary human existence.

Let us go back to that curtain in the opening story. It is said that God looks at history and the earth and each of us individually through that curtain. We are seen in the moment when we were conceived in the eye of God (called our "Original Face" in Buddhism) and simultaneously in the moment we are right here and now and in all the possibilities of what still might be, depending on what we do in this instance...and the next...until we die and enter whatever forever might be. Listening to our own bodies and to the bodies of others is using our ears and our eyes and all our bodies to glean what we were born into as human life, and to touch what our bodies and lives are now, and to grow in "wisdom, age and grace" (see Luke 2:52) before God and other human beings. In the end, we must say that we are mysteries of flesh and blood, inspirited bodies, down to earth and reaching for the stars—and who knows what we might already be becoming. *Listen Here!*

REFLECTIONS AND PRACTICES

1. List your five senses and try to write a litany of thanksgiving for what each of them does and means to you. How do you listen to each of them? Which one are you the least aware of? Which one do you have difficulty with or tend to belittle?

2. Read the book found in the Earlier (Old) Testament called Song of Songs. What does this tradition and book of the Scriptures reveal about God and about how we love one another using our senses and experiencing our sexuality?

3. How does your body praise God? How does your body reveal what you believe about God to others? Does the belief that your body is holy and matters to God—and that everyone else's body is holy and matters to God—impact how you treat people? Remember the story of the sheep and the goats (see Matt 25:31–46): God takes personally what we do or don't do for the needs of others' bodies as though we did or we refused to do that for God.

10

LISTENING TO THE EARTH— TO THE UNIVERSE

We bear the universe in our being as the universe bears us in its being.

—Thomas Berry

The reason why the universe is eternal is that it does not live for itself, it gives life to others as it transforms.

—Lao Tzu

We are children of the universe and we dwell on this floating planet with about seven billion (give or take a couple of hundred million) other human beings in the beginning of the twenty-first century AD. But the universe has been around for eons, and we are very new to the neighborhood. How do we begin to talk about the universe and its "age"? Scientists say it's about 13.7 billion years old and galaxies popped up around ten billion years ago—our own galaxy, sun, moon, and solar system maybe five billion years ago (day four of the creation story). Our earth appeared around 4.6 billion years ago and stabilized around 2.5 billion years ago (day 3). Life on earth—living cells—appeared about 3.5 billion years ago, and life in the sea about 550 million years ago (day 5). Somewhere much later along the lines of time, human beings appeared—about 2.6 million years ago—or maybe as late as just one million years ago. In fact, the first human female from whom all human DNA can be traced is from 160,000 years ago.

There is a marvelous museum in South Africa that presents this timeline, and as you walk along it, the human mind and imagination is staggered. *Homo sapiens* and the use of language appeared just eighty thousand years ago! Egypt rose in power 4,500 years ago, and Abraham and the patriarchs and matriarchs at just about the same time, 2,000 BC. The city of Rome was founded about 2,700 years ago. This timeline keeps being updated by scientists, theologians, and all sorts of people looking at their disciplines and seeing their development in relation to the universe's conception and movement forward (and backward).

People were startled by Edwin Hubble's 1923 discovery that other galaxies existed outside our own Milky Way. Most scientists believed that our galaxy was the extent of the universe! He was watching the stars, and he discovered one in particular (later called a Cepheid variable—a star that vibrates and pulsates and is incredibly bright) in the constellation of Andromeda. In his work, he realized that this star was 800,000 light years away from Earth—more than eight times the distance of the farthest star in the Milky Way. What had looked like "a cloud of gas" was actually another galaxy. This one was the first of twenty-three more galaxies that he found. With his discovery, it began to dawn on all those watching "out there" that we are but a tiny speck in the Milky Way, and the galaxy we float in is just a collection of tiny clusters of stars.

More recently, in November 2013, another galaxy "far, far away" was discovered. It's 13.1 billion light years away from Earth, and it blew into space when the universe was only 700 million years old. It is said to be the most distant galaxy, yet it was spotted by both the Hubble Telescope and one perched on the summit of Mauna Kea, Hawaii. So, we human beings on this tiny planet continue to try to find out how old the universe is—though most astronomers think that we do not have the technology to do that until the next generation devises new spectroscopy and facilities that can move closer to the "birth" of the universe.

In some ways, this knowledge can dwarf the sense of who we are as human beings, and yet if we learn to shift our perspectives and senses to see the design and magnificence of creation, it can stretch our sense of who we are immeasurably. There have been scientists, poets, and theologians who have sensed what a view from the vastness, beauty, and reach of the universe might mean for human beings' understanding of themselves. Seeing "within" things can stretch consciousness and change our place in the universe. In visiting Tintern Abbey years ago, I read the lines of William Wordsworth:

A motion and a spirit, that impels
All thinking things, all objects of all thought,
And rolls through all things.[1]

This sense or possibility of communion or connection with all things has been believed, hoped for, and studied for generations. I once heard it referred to as "the secret soul," and these words of a Sanskrit aphorism, copied from a scrap of paper on the wall of a prayer room in Bangkok reads, "God sleeps in minerals, awakens in plants, walks in animals, and thinks in humans." There was no name or source, but since it was written in Sanskrit, its roots are ancient. This is to begin to speak of human consciousness that draws in all of creation on our singular planet, then pushes us to speak of a consciousness that can also include the vast and, as yet, unknowable reaches of our universe.

We now know that we, our human bodies, are made of the "stuff" of the universe, that our matter is that of the stars.

The nitrogen in our DNA, the calcium in our teeth, the iron in our blood, the carbon in our apple pies were made in the interiors of collapsing stars. We are made of starstuff.

—Carl Sagan

So the question has arisen—can the thousands of millions of cells in our brains and bodies evolve consciousness? Pierre Teilhard de Chardin (1881–1955), a paleontologist, scientist, philosopher, theologian, Jesuit priest, and many believe, a mystic, who loved all of creation and humanity and took seriously the vocation of seeing both as holy, and deepening and expanding its holiness, was intent on discovering the universe from within. In one of his first essays, he wrote,

> There is neither spirit nor matter in the world; the stuff of the universe is spirit-matter. No other substance but this could produce the human molecule.[2]

For Teilhard, this phenomenon of consciousness has been seeded in the universe from the very beginning. Spirit and matter are complementary aspects of reality—he called them "The Within of Things" and "The Without," two sides of one entity. It is as though all that exists has two faces. Simplistically, scientists and many people study the without—the outer face, while others such as theologians, and artists study the within—the inner face.

Others have sought to put this succinctly: "It would be most satisfactory of all if physics and psyche could be seen as complementary aspects of the same reality."
—Wolfgang Pauli[3]

Teilhard later with others discovered in an expedition to Mongolia's Ordos Desert the first sure evidence of Paleolithic humans in that area of the world. It was also where he wrote his "Mass Upon the World," which blends science and mysticism—both his passions in prose and poetry that is liturgical praise par excellence. One of his friends, Julian Huxley, sought to sum up what Teilhard tried to do with his life—and succeeded perhaps beyond his hopes:

> Through this combination of wide scientific knowledge with deep religious feeling...he has forced theologians to view their ideas in the new perspective of evolution, and scientists to see the spiritual implications of that knowledge. He has both clarified and unified our vision of reality. By the light of that new comprehension, it is no longer possible to maintain that science and religion must operate in thought-tight compartments or concern separate sectors of life; they are both relevant to the whole of human experience.[4]

Teilhard's lectures, work, and the strong responses to his ideas led to the institutions of the Church banning him from teaching, and his superiors sent him back to China where he had spent time only 3 years earlier, away from academia and the scientific community, so that he would reflect on his "dangerous thoughts." But it was in China that he drew together his thoughts, and they later became the published versions of *The Phenomenon of Man* and

The Divine Milieu (both of which are good places to begin
reading his thoughts). They were crafted in 1927 and
1930, but not published until 1957 and later.

He created the word *Cosmogenesis* to talk about the
interrelatedness of the cosmos (the universe and everything in it), evolution, and the seed of consciousness
that from the first instant of its emergence is in motion,
unfolding and becoming, creating from within what we
view from without, was headed toward human consciousness from its inception, and is developing toward
a higher consciousness in human beings. He called it a
process of complexification or complexity-consciousness.
That moment is the Omega point that all creation is
moving toward. His spirituality described this point as
God's ingenious creation that is constantly changing
and evolving—we (everything in the universe) are moving toward communion with and union with God. Today
this phenomenon is being further developed by such scientists and theologians as Thomas Berry, Ilia Delio, and
Brian Swimme.

Teilhard died on Easter, April 10, 1955, still silenced
by the Church authorities, and he is buried in Pough-
keepsie, New York. A friend who gave me my first copy
of his *Mass on the World* wrote in the opening blank page
a line from the Book of Revelation 22:13: "I am the Alpha
and the Omega, the First and the Last, the Beginning and
The End." Along with this line, he wrote, "Teilhard
believed that Alpha was the divine spark at the heart of
matter and that in every single atom and particle of the
universe is the Christ-seed. The Omega is the end of our
journey, the direction and arc of evolution and by grace,

our union with God and all that has been created. We are inspirited matter, sanctified to our core and called to be essentially holy and one. From one divine spark to another, let us continue this amazing journey."[5]

We move from the outer edges of the universe back to our planet Earth and our place on this spinning top. How do we listen to the universe, to earth and nature? We begin with an exhortation to listen—to start to listen, with the words of Walt Whitman:

> The earth is rude, silent, incomprehensible at first,
> Nature is rude and incomprehensible at first.
> Be not discouraged, keep on,
> there are divine things well envelop'd,
> I swear to you there are divine things
> more beautiful than words can tell.[6]

On my first trip to Australia to work with the aboriginal peoples there more than two decades ago, one of the first stories I was told is called "Listening to the Voice of the Earth." It was my first gift from the people. They told me it would help me understand the "dream time" that was like a map imprinted over time upon their bodies and brains that was a source of their survival and knowledge of their world as well as their awe and gratefulness for all creation. I was told that I was to listen to all the earth and its creatures if I was to understand them and their ancient ways of living, for their Ancestor spoke to them in all things (*Ancestor* being their word for the Creator-God). The story is told because they weren't always obedient or faithful to the words of their

Ancestor—and they aren't always faithful now either. But this is how it was in the Beginnings.

Once upon a time, it was in the walking and knowing time, the Ancestor spoke to all the peoples every day! The people would rise and immediately go and gather before a great gum tree. They would settle themselves on the ground and listen. It would take a bit of time. They were yawning and awakening. Some would come late, slow to rise. Mothers would feed their children and there would be the sound of suckling, and fathers would quiet their children, telling them how to be still and listen to the breeze and the smells in the air and to their own hearts. There would be the sound of coughs, sighs, and movement as everyone got comfortable on the ground. Often someone would begin with a hum, and that would draw them closer together. And the Ancestor would speak. Each would hear the voice. All heard a piece of wisdom. When the Ancestor had finished speaking for that day, the people would turn to one another, some sharing what they heard right away. Others would speak as the day unfolded. Some would not speak until another day, or when the Ancestor's words were needed. This was the way.

But with time, there were those who didn't come. They didn't want to get up so early. They didn't want to spend that time with all the others, and then wait to see who would speak. They began to say that they didn't hear anything and didn't see anything but a gum tree and whatever the weather was that day. As the days were continued, fewer and fewer of the people came to sit on the earth and listen to the Ancestor in the gum tree. They dwindled down to a few old ones and a few young ones. They began, instead, to listen to what they thought as they worked or overheard from others or were busy about their tasks and all they had to do to eat, and harvest the sea and the desert and take care of building houses and carrying water. The voice was not stilled, but no one was there to listen, to heed it, or to share it with the others. The earth began to change. It dried up. There were no winds to cool and ease. The plants shriveled and did not return. Even the birds did not sing or make noises. The tides shifted. Storms came harder and more often. It was hotter—then it was colder. Food was scarce and the people began to mistrust one another. It seemed like not only the earth was sick and dying, but the people were sick and dying too.

One person came again to sit early in the morning in front of the gum tree and remained. Others joined her, the children and the elders first. Then whole families began the return and soon the whole village. They sat in the quiet and listened again. They sought to hear the wind, anything that moved, the sound of water, their own hearts, and the emanations of those around them. It was hard. They couldn't hear anything. They wondered if the Ancestor was displeased with them and if the Ancestor had left them in their misery and struggle. They needed a word. After many days, their hope was answered and they all heard the voice of the Ancestor again. As they sat before the gum tree, they all sensed this would be the last time Ancestor spoke in words, but Ancestor would give them a sign that the voice would always be there, around, with them and in them. As they sat there, the tree split open before them, from top to bottom, a great light coming down the inside of its trunk; then the tree closed up again. There was stillness that was full and moving everywhere.

They say, that since then, all the people, the Aborigines know that the Ancestor speaks to them through every part of the world, all of earth and what lives here, the seas and movements of seasons, the day and night, the heavens and what lives and moves above them. But, it is their place to gather together and sit on the earth under the sky and listen daily—or again all of nature and we ourselves will shrivel up, and we will be sick and the dying will come sooner. Listen.

I love the story and love to tell it. Just the sound of it being shared and listened to seems to carry something almost tangible that everyone senses and takes to heart, speaking and reflecting on it. If possible, after the telling, everyone goes outside to practice listening. After about ten minutes on their own, they gather on the ground, no matter the weather, and begin to learn to listen together. Once, when I did this in an interfaith gathering, someone gave me a handwritten quote that he wanted to share from his tradition. It read, "Today, at sundown we will mark the beginning of Rosh Hashanah, the beginning of our Jewish new year. For us it is a time of reflection, of gratitude for all that has been lavishly given by the Master of the Universe in the past year and we are encouraged to make resolutions for this new year—for our souls, our families, our communities and all that has been made. We are told to remember—there is no place where God is not!"

Those words are reiterated in story after story from all the major religious traditions of our world. The Navajo shared an anonymous poem with me—they say it is wisdom born of long experience. "Know things in nature—all are like a person. Talk to tornadoes; talk to the thunder, they are your friends and will protect you." Definitely, in this time of climate change, global warming, and the reality of stronger storms that come upon us around the world, this is good medicine—necessary advice that we might begin to heed immediately. Joe Bruchac, an Abenaki from upstate New York, made it even plainer with his words: "We need to walk to know sacred places, those around us and those within. We need to walk to remember the songs."

Not one single atom opposes us.
—Zen Master Hongzhi

Human generosity is possible only because at the center of the solar system a magnificent stellar generosity pours forth free energy day and night without stop and without complaint and without the slightest hesitation. This is the way of the universe. This is the way of life.
—Brian Swimme

But if we look around at our world, it is not all one of beauty, harmony, and fecundity. Our psalms and songs proclaim that everything in the universe praises

God, that the heavens continue to tell the glory of God, and that the first book of revelation that God ever wrote is that of the natural world, its seasons and weathers, its long faithfulness, and continual development. But even as we discover myriad life forms—the latest treasure trove being the depths of the oceans that scientists are descending into and photographing for the first time— we would have to be blind and deaf not to notice that the ground we walk upon, the air we breathe, the food we eat, and the waters we drink are now polluted, laced with chemicals, acids, and carcinogens. There are end- less studies of the amount of destruction yearly, even monthly in the ozone layer above us and the melting of fresh water in our ice caps at either end of our planet.

The most recent Red List from the International Union for Conservation of Nature reports that 869 species have gone extinct due to human activity in the last five-hundred years. Statistics: it includes a quarter of all mammals; one in eight birds; one third of all amphib- ians; and two-thirds of all the plants in the world. The earth we live on, the places we dwell in, are being destroyed at a fantastically increasing rate—all around us. We are at a point in the consciousness and survival of human beings and the earth that we must become aware of our surroundings and change our attitudes and behaviors toward all on earth that is not two-legged, not a human being. In the Qur'an it is written, "Allah asks: 'The heavens and the earth and all in between, thinkest thou I make them in jest?'" From our lack of considera- tion of most of the world we live in and the extent to which we are destroying the basic necessities of life along with animals, birds, what lives in the sea, and every manner of insect that wings its way through the air, we care nothing for anything but ourselves. We must begin to heed the insight and wisdom necessary for survival that leaders around the world are beginning to repeat over and over again. The Dalai Lama tries to insert this line in many of his teachings, no matter the topic: "Today, more than ever before, life must be characterized by a sense of universal responsibility, not only nation to nation, and human to human, but also human to other forms of life."

The world and its elements: earth (ground), water, air, fire, (wood is included as the fifth element in China) are disintegrating around us, and we are using our basic resources with no thought of tomorrow, let alone our children and the next generation of human beings. The climate is changing radically, the number and intensity of catastrophic storms is increasing, bringing with them not just the obliteration of the earth and everything in their path, but staggering numbers of deaths and misery. We could pen a litany of places now gone forever—nonexistent—along with species that are now extinct. These are not statistics. Each number is a human being and a life bound to so many others, now gone, leaving behind so many others broken, maimed, terrified, and desolate.

At the recent International Climate Conference held in Warsaw in 2013, the delegate from the Philippines who was from the city of Tacloban, the place hardest hit and almost completely wiped out—along with more than six-thousand of its people—went on a public fast, trying to emphasize the immediacy and reality of what is called global warming that is altering every area of weather and affecting the majority and the poorest of people we share this planet with. He was fasting until the conference acted—moved beyond discussion, bickering over whether or not this phenomenon of global climate change even existed, and resistance because of any action that might have economic consequences on the richest nations, which contribute the most to the acceleration of the changes. Deb Sano spoke, pleading for people to hear and listen to his testimony, to hear with their hearts (wills) and consciences.

To anyone who continues to deny the reality of climate change, I dare them to go to the islands of the Pacific, the islands of the Caribbean, and the islands of the Indian Ocean and see the effects of rising sea levels; to the mountainous regions of the Himalayas and the Andes to see communities confronting glacial floods; to the Arctic, where communities grapple with the fast dwindling polar ice caps; to the large deltas of the Mekong, the Ganges, the Amazon, and the Nile, where lives and livelihoods are drowned; to the hills of Central America that confront similar monstrous hurricanes; to the vast savannas of Africa, where climate change has likewise become a matter of life and death, as food and water becomes scarce. Not to forget the massive hurricanes in the Gulf of Mexico and the eastern seaboard of North America—if that is not enough, there is similar destructive weather in the Pacific now, affecting the Philippines and other countries in the region.

Pieces of our world are being wiped out, erased. How long will the coastlands exist; how much land will disappear or turn to desert; how long can we survive on the shrinking amount of fresh water in the world? There was generally for thousands and thousands of years about 6 percent of the world's water that was available to drink—fresh water. We are now down to less than 2 percent of that remaining, as it disappears at a rate unprecedented in human history.

Jesus speaks of whole towns that will disappear because they will not respond to his words—to the reality of the presence of the kingdom, the realm of God on earth. He reminds everyone that not only will individuals be judged, but whole towns and nations will be judged on what they chose to do or what they chose to ignore or reject. It is an image of Jesus as prophet, as truth-teller, exhorting people to change now, before it is too late.

> Then he began to reproach the towns where most of his mighty deeds had been done, since they had not yet repented. Woe to you, Chorazin! Woe to you, Bethsaida! For if the mighty deeds done in your midst had been done in Tyre and Sidon, they would long ago have repented in sackcloth and ashes. But I tell you, it will be more tolerable for Tyre and Sidon on the day of judgment than for you. (Matt 11:20–22)

We can easily ignore such words and reduce them to acceptance of Jesus' teaching thousands of years ago—and having nothing to do with anything that we are speaking about—or can we? The mighty deeds that God has done—the part of creation each of us dwells in; the cities we have built, the neighborhoods we move into; the choices we make about open spaces, national parks (and the reality that we even have been reduced to portioning out wild places). Our economy, our wars, our business decisions touting development and crass principles regarding the use of our resources based solely on the profit of a few and the destruction of so much—what have we done? What are we doing, continuing to blithely ignore the effects of our way of life, our consumerism, our selfishness and brutality toward the world and most of the rest of the human race? We most certainly deserve to fall into the peoples of Chorazin and Bethsaida. Worse still is the reality that the nations contributing the most to global destruction, pollution, and climate change all are intent on calling themselves Christian nations. Jesus continues, "And you [spoken in relation to Capernaum, the place Jesus made his base and home—all of us now] 'Will you be exalted to heaven? You will go down to the netherworld.' For if the mighty deeds done in your midst had been done in Sodom, it would have remained until this day. But I tell you, it will be more tolerable for the land of Sodom on the day of judgment than for you" (Matt 11:23–24).

Whole towns and regions are disappearing, becoming barren and uninhabitable. Metro Manila was one of a number of major cities in the world that was declared "uninhabitable" more than fifteen years ago by World Watch. It is our doing, as we refuse to acknowledge what is happening and our part in this destruction that will only continue to worsen and spread across our world. Jesus tells a parable earlier in the Gospel about those who build on sand and those who build on rock—the wise and the fools. It can serve as the basis of our necessity to act together and begin to respond to the calamitous reality that we are living in the midst of daily.

> Everyone who listens to these words of mine and acts on them will be like a wise man [woman] who built his house on rock. The rain fell, the floods came, and the winds blew and buffed the house. But it did not collapse; it had been set solidly on rock. And everyone who listens to these words of mine but does not act on them will be like a fool who built his house on sand. The rain fell, the floods came and the winds blew and buffeted the house. And it collapsed and was completely ruined. (Matt 7:24–26)

Brutal, stark, and demanding as Jesus' words are, they are nonetheless our only two choices: we must repent, we must act, and we must act together immediately or we shall all be completely ruined. We must begin now to listen and look to another way of being on earth and dwelling in this fragile and precious world of ours that we have been entrusted with by the Creator. We must take to heart the words of Arundhati Roy, a writer and activist who speaks on behalf of many people working to preserve water and stop the building of hydroelectric dams across the middle of India when she

says in her rallying cry, "Not only is another world possible, she is on her way. On a quiet day; I can hear her
breathing." We live on hope and hope drives us to make
what we believe reality, being willing to do all in our
power with others to give birth to that reality, being
bearers of life, being midwives to that life, and yet, perhaps never experiencing its fullness in our lifetime. It
will be our gift to those who come after us.

Any spirituality or way of life that is practiced now
and in the future must take into consideration the vital
and immediate necessity of radically altering our awareness of the earth, the universe and our place in it, as well
as our responsibility to care for it and preserve it, living
in communion with it, not destroying it and using it for
our own ends, no matter the cost and effect on our present and futures. We must do more than pray and talk
about what needs to be done; we must begin to listen
with our hearts (wills) and put into practice what is
demanded if we are to have an earth worth living on—
all too soon.

The Patriarch Bartholomew, the Ecumenical Patriarch
of Constantinople, is often called the Green Patriarch
because of his theology and preaching over the last
decades on environmental issues. In his Message to the
Nineteenth Session of the Conferences of the Parties in
Warsaw, 2013 (the same one the Philippine delegate
spoke to), he had much to say in a few words to those
attending and to all of us. It began with the human
crisis as an existing reality—get beyond any talk of
whether it exists or not—and got immediately to the
reality of the need to face the consequences of our

choices and behavior—all the nations and peoples—over the last decades and during our long history. He began with asking the question of what does preserving the planet have to do with saving souls and if the question of global climate change and the exploitation of our nature's resources are matters better attended to by politicians, scientists, those involved in technology and government, and business. After all, aren't these worldly things as opposed to what is sacred and more important? Underlying his remarks are crucial issues. Is the horror and destruction of the earth and human life the result of our own moral evil and choices? Is this reality sin?—mortal sin that is the result of many other serious sins that are committed and adopted as systematic structures of evil that are versions of selfishness, greed, violence, avarice, pride, and other practices that are evil? Perhaps even to continue to demand that we separate what is of the world from what is of individual human is wrong. He said,

> There are no two ways of looking at either the world or God. There is no distinction between concern for human welfare and concern for ecological preservation. The way we relate to nature as creation directly reflects the way we believe in God as Creator of all things. The sensitivity with which we handle the natural environment clearly mirrors the sacredness that we reserve for the divine.

Moreover, scientists estimate that those who will be most hurt by global warming in the years to come are those who can least afford it. According to the Gospel of Matthew, the questions that will be asked of us all at the final moment of accountability will not be about our religious observance but on whether we fed the hungry, gave drink to the thirsty, clothed the naked, comforted the sick, and cared for captives.

Our reckless consumption of the earth's resources—energy, water, and forests—threatens us with irreversible climate change. Burning more fuel than we need in an overpopulated city, we may contribute to droughts or floods thousands of miles away.

To restore the planet, we need a spiritual worldview that brings frugality and simplicity, humility and respect. We must constantly be aware of the impact of our actions on all of creation. We must direct our focus away from what we want to what the planet needs. We must choose to care for creation; otherwise, we do not really care about anything at all.

In our efforts to contain global warming, we are admitting just how unprepared we are to sacrifice some of our selfish and greedy lifestyle. When will we learn to say, "Enough!"? When will we understand how important it is to leave as light a footprint as possible on this planet for the sake of future generations? The time to choose is now.

In the classic theological response to what needs to be done, there is a process: confession of wrong doing and collusion with evil, naming our sin; radically altering behavior—stopping some things and incorporating new practices—doing restorative justice together that seeks to undo some of the violence and harm that was done in the practice of evil—these are the core elements of repentance, so that we can once again reconcile ourselves to others and our environment and hope to atone for what we have dis-created—to live at-one again. It means to reverse the process by acting singularly and together in as many varied groups as we belong to in such ways that we once again create life ever more abundantly, protect life and all that is needed to sustain life. Otherwise, our hearts are barren and dead, as barren and dead as the earth we are pushing toward such extremes of violence, extinction, and destruction. The reverence we have shown and practice toward what we contain in our churches—sacraments, bread and wine, even statues, icons, the buildings we meet in, candles, and what we, in the past, considered to be holy relics, sacred and powerful—we must now extend to all in the world, all that has been created, and all that is an expression of our God.

Our spirituality and our lives must reflect that we believe that everything that God created is good, is very good, is sacred and holy: beginning with human beings but moving out into all else. Ernesto Cardenal in one of his exhortations and prayers wrote:

> God's signature is on the whole of nature... they are outbursts of love. The whole of nature is bursting with love, set in it by God, who is love, to kindle the fire of love in us. All things have no other reason for existing, no other meaning....
>
> Nature is like God's shadow, reflecting God's beauty and splendor....God's fingerprints are

upon every particle matter....And my body was also made for the love of God. Every cell in my body is a hymn to my creator and a declaration of love. As the Kingfisher was made to fish and the humming bird to suck nectar from flowers, so we are made for the contemplation and love of God.[7]

Here we are on this constantly moving, spinning, and shining planet of ours, children of the universe. Along with the entire universe, we are here to simply contemplate, sing the praises of the Creator, and live in communion with all that has been, is, and will be by grace and the will of the Holy. Thomas Merton began to set this in motion as a first step when he wrote, "Contemplative living is living in true relationship with oneself, God, others and nature; free of the illusions of separateness." We speak of contemplation as "a long loving look at reality" but what if contemplation is just as surely "a long loving listening to all that exists, especially what is hard to listen to, alone and with others, that drives us to be united compassionately in God with all that God has created"?[8]

There is a marvelous Jewish midrash about the time immediately after the creation of the world, when God asked the angels what they thought of what he had set in motion. They were overawed but also said, "There is one thing that is missing." They asked God, "Where is the sound of praise? After all, we here in heaven praise you continuously. Why doesn't the world you made do it as well?" God looked at the angels and said, "Ah, that is something you don't understand or know—but the human beings I have made do—everything I have made praises me. Listen to the sounds—the birds twittering and making music; the sound of waters, oceans, rain, wind in the trees, all that murmurs, rustles, trills, croaks, roars, whispers, hums, speaks, sighs, laughs, cries, sings—there is nothing that does not praise me. You must learn a deeper and truer way of praise by listening to everything I have made and continue to make." Listen!

It seems that God is always listening, not just to us but to all that has been made. How deaf we all are to what is right around us as well as the universal harmonies and melodies, symphonies and sounds. What have we never heard that delights God always, all ways? Let us begin to live: listen—do we hear what God hears? *Listen Here!*

REFLECTIONS AND PRACTICES

1. Research an animal, bird, or sea creature that has become extinct and mourn its passing. What could it have revealed to us of God's goodness? Share it with others and learn from what they discover, find, and lose.

2. Try writing a prayer for the more than seven billion people on the earth right now, and begin to pray as a child of this wide expanse of people here on earth.

3. "There is a way that nature speaks, that land speaks. Most of the time we are simply not patient enough, quiet enough to pay attention to the story." (Linda Hogan)

Find a place—one you love, or near where you live, within walking distance—and go and listen to the place, the land, that piece of ground and ecosystem. Have patience and wait and listen. Return again and again so that you begin to hear its story and become attached to it. Listen through your body, sitting on the earth, climbing into a tree—however.

11

LISTENING IN RELATIONSHIPS OF UNEQUAL POWER

"Real listening is a willingness to let the other person change you."

—Alan Alda[1]

In the process of completing this book I did a number of retreats and workshops with chaplains in the military, priests from a number of dioceses, and others involved in spiritual direction and counseling. Many asked that I address the issue of listening when one person has more power than the other person. This issue would inevitably surface as a real need for all of them, no matter what other areas of listening we were discussing. The experience of such situations was described as troubling, difficult, and stressful. The issues of responsibility and accountability were foremost—especially for those whose power impacted the other's life, both immediately and long-term.

This situation of inequality exists in various situations on a number of significant levels. For those in a work relationship where one is the "boss" or "superior," the inequality impacted promotion, economic stability, and daily work. This is also true in military situations, where the psychological and religious power of being a chaplain operating on a personal level is coupled with the inequality of military rank. (Chaplains in all branches of military service enter as officers and so are ranked above enlisted personnel.) For priests (and bishops, deacons, and religious men and women in various parish, diocesan, and vocational positions), power imbalance is intensified by the symbolism of their specific "religious" affiliations with a church or denomination, as well as their being a mediator between the person and their God.

All had questions and even difficulties with boundaries on how to listen, respond, question, and resolve (to whatever degree possible) the issue at hand apart from their own position of authority.

This chapter deals with each position—that of the person with less power and the person who has more. Beginning with the one in a position of less power, we will look at the following:

1. Does the person come asking for a favor, perceiving a need, or wanting something from the other person?

2. Does the person come wanting to be related to as an equal?

3. Does the person come intending or needing to speak to their superior regarding their difficulties with them?

Each of these situations presents a different set of skills. We will also look at the reality of the one with more power to effect change economically, promotion-wise, as well as more personally within the relationship, but who can also heed the insights that are offered for their own change and action.

FROM BELOW

"Position in life is everything."
—common wisdom from Nana

It is helpful to remember that every person has power. This power is held deeply within—it is the essence of the person bound to their very soul, personality, and being. In what we are considering here, we acknowledge these powers of all human beings, but focus instead on the power found in institutions, be they religious, military, educational, professional, or societal.

These initial suggestions are for all involved, no matter one's relative position. Let's look first from the point of view of one approaching a stronger person, especially as the petitioner: one asking a favor, or dealing with a problem. These realities are foundational for all such encounters—in seeking to be treated as an equal and in attempting to describe or approach an issue that is directed at the one with more power and authority.

Let's begin with a mental image: porcupines! In some ways each of us is a porcupine and in many of our dealings with each other you can see the difficulties involved with two porcupines trying to get closer. There is a learned distance/nearness that is crucial to any encounter. This comfort zone is all the more important when there is a porcupine and a cat or a dog or any other smaller animal. The first thing to remember is that the quills of the porcupine are NOT meant for attack but for protection. They are kept in check until threatened and then they have to be "launched." We all have quills we use to keep our distance and maintain a sense of security. When we deal with others who are stronger and more powerful than ourselves, we often immediately go into "on alert" mode, and maybe even engage "attack" mode. So, before we approach anyone in authority we have to be sure we secure our quills. This can be done before the encounter by talking over what we intend to discuss with someone we trust, or by sitting quietly to think through what we are trying to express and planning out what we want to say, how to say it, and considering the other person's possible responses.

Think also about how salmon deal with upstream currents when they return to their home grounds to spawn. I have often stood on a bridge overlooking a weir watching runs of salmon make their way upstream—launching themselves into the air, as though defying gravity and hitting smack-hard the water as they land. As they soar into the air, they turn their undersides belly up all along their length so they hit the current flat on, squarely. It is that slap, that front-on encounter with the water that lifts them and throws them farther up the water current. They do this again and again, moving farther and farther along their return path. They face the water not as an obstacle but as a jumping-off place and point of meeting the next step or piece of their journey. To anyone watching they seem to be flying as much as swimming!

These two images reveal the balance needed when one person engages with another who has more authority and seeks to be listened to, understood, and responded to. It is like walking a tightrope—if you lean too far to the right you usually fall on your head; if you lean too far to the left you usually fall on your behind. You must constantly shift to remain stable and remember to focus on your goal—where you're going. When you are the one speaking, look at the person and remember what you are seeking to share and ask of them.

Parallel to this balancing act, the second reality to keep in mind is knowing your own borders. We must walk a line between honesty and vulnerability—knowing what to say and what to refrain from saying. Again, it helps to even write out what you want to say and the end point that you are hoping for in return. This way of communicating is about keeping your self-respect and affords the same degree of respect to the person with power over you. We have to learn to speak so the other can better discern the situation at hand and what it is you are asking of them—treading carefully yet confidently. We use language and tone of voice differently with different people—whether business, friendship, casual, religious, or more formal language—and we are usually more comfortable with one or another.

Choosing what and what not to share is as critical as choosing knives when cooking. One type of knife works best on fish and an altogether different one is better with vegetables. One chooses how transparent one needs to be with the other, walking that line between clarifying one's position and keeping extraneous material at a bare minimum. In situations of inequality, it is easy to mistakenly allow in feelings related to other issues in our lives not connected to the situation at hand. It is partly the responsibility of the one with less power to be clear and not change the interaction by what is shared. There is honesty and there is transparency or vulnerability. Honesty is sharing information only as needed and feelings that are *your own feelings*—not feelings directed at the person with whom you are attempting to communicate. Transparency is often a question of depth and breadth—how much you share rather than what you share. Usually, the more transparent one is the more emotional one can become. In turn, one might expect the listener to also be more responsive on an emotional level.

If we are in need, approaching another for a favor, advice, or to address a particular issue, we need to choose our language more practically and adhere more closely to society's expectations of behavior. A story from the Gospel of Mark can help us see what this looks like for the petitioner who is asking someone with the power to respond.

A leper came to him [and kneeling down] begged him, saying: "If you wish, you can make me clean." Moved with pity, he stretched out his hand, touched him, and said to him, "I do will it. Be made clean." The leprosy left him immediately, and he was made clean. Then, warning him sternly, he dismissed him at once. Then he said to him, "See that you tell no one anything, but go, show yourself to the priest and offer for your cleansing what Moses pre-scribed; that will be proof for them." The man went away and began to publicize the whole matter. He spread the report abroad so that it was impossible for Jesus to enter a town openly. He remained outside in deserted places, and people kept coming to him from every-where. (Mark 1:40–45)

The leper is definitely someone with less power, espe-cially in relation to Jesus. Lepers were required to keep their distance from others in public (hence the need for Jesus to stretch out his hand in order to be able to touch this person) and his language reflects his need and respect for Jesus' authority. Most probably he knelt to offer his request, physically accepting that power. Even today, there are protocols we commonly recognize as appropriate when requesting something from the other person. This may involve making an appointment to meet at a certain type of venue (an office, a private room), at a particular time (business hours, at the other's convenience), and even the type of greeting that is exchanged when the meeting takes place. The request is then posited as a simple statement of the need.

In just this way, the leper expresses his need simply and with dignity. The "begging" is found first in his actual request—as a leper—and in his acknowledgement of Jesus' power, ability, or choice whether or not to respond as the leper so desperately hopes and wants. Jesus explains that his intent, his will is about life ever more abundant (in Jesus' words from John's Gospel) and that he declares his decision a command. Then he gives the cured leper two tasks that he is to do in response. The first is that he is NOT to broadcast what Jesus has done for him, and second, he must show himself to the priest so that the societal and religious expectations are fulfilled. In the same way, many of our relationships are meant to be kept between just the two of us, kept private and not publicly aired. Many (if not most) one-on-one encounters that entail speaking/hearing/listening are not for outside discussion.

This helps us to look at a conversation between two persons when one is operating out of lesser power. A short quote from the poet E. E. Cummings can situate what this encounter can look like and how it can operate.

> We do not believe in ourselves until someone reveals that something deep inside us is valuable, worth listening to, worthy of our trust, sacred to our touch. Once we believe in ourselves we can risk curiosity, wonder, spontaneous delight of any experience that reveals the human spirit.[2]

What if the person with limited power wants to be accepted as an equal? This kind of communication might best be described as "dialogue"—a more balanced acceptance of the power each person possesses in the relationship. Again, the person approaching the other in authority has to begin by taking responsibility for their own agenda and what they say and intend to communicate. There will be differences of opinion or perceptions of the situation, or one side may have more information than the other person—on both sides of the conversation and meeting. It is hard not to become focused only on our ideas and opinions and on convincing the other person to agree, rather than being satisfied with simply stating our aim so that the other understands.

This kind of dialogue begins with some acknowledgement of shared interest or a shared understanding that nothing specific is expected. What you want to share needs to be stated clearly at the outset. As before, it helps if we examine our own assumptions beforehand and understand what it is we are trying to communicate. Dialogue is not about convincing or even about changing another's mind. It's about hearing...listening to the other and becoming aware of what's happening and what is going on. It is never about debating, taking sides, or deciding one is right and one is wrong. It is about seeking connections and what possibilities exist in the present and what might be hoped for in the future.

Listening in this manner can be found in a variety of relationships: teachers and students, bosses and workers, counselors and counselees, chaplains and seekers. These encounters are mutual forays into understanding the other and not exercises in judgment. These encounters involve sharing confidences, struggling with experiences, dealing with shared situations of conflict, work, and relationships that can be helpful in places of work and life.

Jewish philosopher Martin Buber described this kind of encounter in his book *I and Thou*,[3] saying that there are two primary ways one can relate to one another—as I and Thou or as I and It. The first is founded on respect, appreciation, and listening with openness of mind, heart, and one's self. The second is based on one's own selfishness, sense of power, and keeps one from being open to the other person on levels of mind and heart. The second lacks a good deal of basic respect, honesty, and compassion and tends to view the other person as an object rather than someone deserving of respect.

This kind of unequal power-base relating is open to a shift in the relationship and can be nurtured either in one-on-one connections or in a small group that meets to share not just information, but goals, methods, and background that can be helpful, even feelings and personal experiences that can lend insight and understanding to shared situations that might arise. Again, it might be helpful to return to the idea of the porcupines! This story is taken from many stories collected from northern Vancouver, British Columbia and many of the First Nations' understandings of communication. Even though it is a story for children, it is nonetheless insightful for all ages.

Once upon a time there were two boys, one older than the other. They would often explore the area where they lived together—the beach, the forest's edge, the back streets. One day when they had climbed a hill and were looking out over the fields below, they decided to claim the area as their own and so they assembled a makeshift flag from their bandanas tied to a stick. This would be their turf, their land, their hill. The older boy, planting their flag in the ground, declared, "This is my land and all I can see is mine!" The younger boy immediately protested. "Shouldn't you say, 'This is OUR land,' since we climbed this together?" The elder responded, "No, I'm older, I'm stronger and bigger and so it's mine and I'm going to build a fence to keep others out—including you, when I don't want you around."

Within moments they were struggling over the flag; the younger tried to take it down but the older boy started punching him and shoved him down the hill. At the bottom of the hill the younger boy sat on the ground, crying. On the top of the hill, the older was also sitting, but with self-satisfaction, when he saw a porcupine towards him. Porcupine asked him, "Why is the other boy crying?" "Because," he said, "I hit him and pushed him off my hill. This place is mine and I decide who can be here." Porcupine responded a bit sadly, "You can no more declare the land is yours than you can say the air or the oceans are yours. They belongs to all of us. Look at my quills. They're mine and they protect me like a fence—like the one you want to build. But they also keep others at a distance and away from me—not only those who might want to harm me, but those who want to be my friends or live with me. It isn't good to make fences where they aren't needed. It causes more problems and keeps people from helping you and living with you. You are left on your own."

The older boy listened respectfully and thought, "This is what Porcupine knows because his quills stick out all over, but its also what my younger friend was trying to tell me when he kept saying, 'It's ours.'" So, down the hill he went to talk with his friend so that they might again play and discover new worlds together.

It sounds like a "nice" story, but does it reflect reality? Yes, it actually does. Most disagreements that arise in every type of relationship begin with adamant declarations that begin with "I" and exclude others. Practically every response that will change the reality for the better begins with listening to the other respectfully and seeking out what is "ours" in order to continue what we are attempting to do, working with one another in a larger context. There have to be moments and experiences for both that can shift future encounters. It is the Muslim poet Rumi who says, "Since, in order to speak, one must first hear, do you come to speech by way of hearing?"[4]

The last situation—in which one with less power approaches the person who is more dominant—is, of course, the most difficult and the most unpredictable of meetings. The person initiating this conversation is more vulnerable than usual and has more to lose than the other person. It is incredibly difficult to begin these conversations and be heard if the person in authority hasn't already made some intimation that they are open and care about what others think about them and their positions/jobs and shared goals. The paradigm of power is always there—sometimes clearly evident and other times not. The person on the rung below has to have courage and be careful about why they are bringing up this particular issue and what they hope to gain in return. They have to trust that the person in power actually cares and can benefit from what they have to share. The person raising an issue has to be clear how it impacts others involved and the work being done as well, respectfully describing what happens to them (and others) when the person in power acts as they do. The person seeking to speak to someone in power as an equal has to be clear about their own feelings but NOT rely primarily on those feelings to communicate.

This situation can be described as being a "whistle blower," as being prophetic—sharing what's happening and what is going to happen if things/decisions and people don't change. It is seeking to be a corrective in a volatile situation. One has to weigh the possible consequences with the possibilities of change and being heard before deciding to speak. In many cases, it is the purpose of the conversation that must outweigh the more immediate or present feelings of the one who decides to speak out to the person in authority, whether for oneself or for others.

There are many stories of people who do this and they are—at best—ignored, or they may suffer financially, personally, or even violently. But there are also stories of being heard, of being listened to, and of real change and conversion, both personally and as part of a group and the work the group does. This one is from the Zen tradition—a story told about a child and the head teacher in a monastery.

Once upon a time an orphan was sent to a monastery to live. People kept telling the child, "It's better to be a monk and get some education than starve and be a beggar on the street." After weeks in the monastery, the orphan put on weight and grew stronger and healthier, but everyone could still see that the orphan was miserable and unhappy. Eventually the orphan ran away—but was brought back by the authorities. The child was brought before the head teacher and threatened with expulsion. The teacher asked, "Do you want to be thrown out into the world to freeze or starve to death?" The young one didn't hesitate before blurting out, "I'd rather freeze to death out there than be warm and treated so badly in here!" The teacher froze momentarily, then gathered himself and said, "I know you're not used to the discipline and the life, but you will learn. You will learn the scriptures, how to read and write, and the wisdom of the ancients."

The young one responded, "If you want me to learn, than talk to me of kindness and compassion," then lifted his shirt to show the teacher the scars and bruises from being disciplined. Seeing the tears coursing down the child's face, the teacher was silent and inwardly stung. He had trouble talking but finally managed to say, "Please, give us one more chance." The young one relented and stayed. The teacher had all the sticks used for discipline destroyed and began to teach those who were the teachers to speak softly and encourage the younger ones, and to teach by example with doing what was required with them.

They say the young one stayed fifteen years before leaving and becoming a teacher outside the monastery. They say a new name was given to the one who was now older and wiser—*Kazi*—and word spread that Kazi was the one to listen, to hear disputes, to make peace, to reconcile, to get others to speak again to one another and to listen without bitterness, no matter what the situation entailed. They would say, when they told this story later, that when each side or person had stated their case and what was the issue, Kazi would interrupt and say, "Speak to me of compassion first...and then, more of compassion."[5]

This ends well, but there are many stories told of more destructive and bitter responses. So when someone decides to approach someone in power personally, they must take into consideration whether or not they are willing to accept the consequences that may be unexpected, unplanned, and unwanted. Even in the Scriptures of the Gospels, many conversations that Jesus has with lawyers, teachers, and members of groups such as the Pharisees, scribes, followers of Herod, or wealthy people, end badly—with the others entrenched in their opinions and feelings, their fears and their intent to destroy Jesus. In order to do this sort of speaking and listening one must be wise, crafty, inventive, and compassionate and adept at speaking the truth with respect—and one must hope for the outcome to be graceful.

FROM ABOVE

Siddhartha listened. He was now listening intently, completely absorbed, quite empty, taking in everything. He felt that he had now completely learned the art of listening. He had often heard all of this before, all the numerous voices in the river, but today they sounded different. He could no longer distinguish the different voices....They all belonged to each other: the lament of those that yearn, the laughter of the wise, the cry of indignation and the groan of the dying.

                  —*Siddhartha*, Hermann Hesse

Now to look at the other side of the equation—how to listen when you are the one with the power, the upper hand, the authority and position in relation to those who are "under your authority." In many ways this position is more difficult to speak about than being the one without the authority. From the position below, the major problem is that there are very few instances where those in authority can be held accountable and responsible by those without the power. The power paradigm is tightly structured and broad in scope, and it is assumed by the one in control and often used without integrity or responsibility—often even without awareness that it is being evoked and levied by the one who is dominant.

But what must be stated adamantly and repeatedly over and over again is that the GREATER THE POWER a

person has the GREATER THE RESPONSIBILITY AND
ACCOUNTABILITY they bear in listening and responding
to the person exerting or using their power with integrity
and respect. The structures of authority—in work and
school; as well as in areas of the military, religion, and
counseling; in religious and moral issues and relationships of intimacy; and in sexuality—can result in exclusion, punishment, public shaming, violence, and injustice.
The burden is always greater for the one with more power.

A simple story that can help illustrate this comes
from the Jewish teaching tradition. Once upon a time a
man came to the rabbi desperate and complaining about
his wife. His complaint: she talked constantly about
anything and everything. He had no peace, no
respite...what should he do? The rabbi paused and
answered simply, "LISTEN to every word the woman
says. Do this for months, be attentive to her every word,
and then come back and talk with me." The man obeyed.

Months later he returned and the rabbi questioned
him on how things were going. "Better," the man
replied. "I think I'm beginning to understand what she's
trying to say and what's important." "Good" was the
rabbi's response—"now go back again and LISTEN to
every word she doesn't say and come back again to tell
me how things are going." The man did as the rabbi had
said, though he was slower to come back this time.
"Well, how's it going?" And the man said, "You know I
don't know. I understand her more and she speaks less.
What now?"

The rabbi said, "Have you tried telling her what's
been happening between you and me these past months

and just ask her what she thinks about it all?" Stunned, the man shook his head. "Now, go home and ask her if she is hearing you so that you can begin to listen to one another's hearts together." They say the man did not return; but the rabbi began to wonder himself if he was listening to what those who came to him were really trying to say.

Listening from above or from a base that is not shared by the person trying to be heard always is about more than the words spoken. Do we who have power listen to what is not being said? This is the reason why most people come to us in the first place. We need to be aware of the fact that we are not usually being asked to necessarily fix what they are talking about, but to lead them to their own wisdom and knowing how to respond for themselves. Our use of power—our perceived knowledge, wisdom, and understanding—is not to be used to change them or others, but to reframe their questions and enable them to reflect and learn from their experience what can be done.

Often when I tell this story this way—in the traditional telling—I am questioned about the point of view of the woman in the story. The advice given by the rabbi the first two times the husband comes is, of itself, good but it doesn't even acknowledge that the problem might also be found in the husband—who either doesn't speak at all or doesn't respond to anything the woman says. They say things like the following: perhaps the rabbi needs to learn that any conversation or relationship is with two people and that for any dialogue to actually happen, both need to be involved. If the rabbi is to go beyond merely responding to the man's initial complaint and problem (which the man located in the other person, his wife), then the rabbi needs to come at listening "sideways" or from "underneath" what is being said. It's a marvelous concept. It is listening under/over/around/in and through the words and from outside the initial phrasing of what is posited. This is a kind of listening that anyone in a position of power meeting another one-on-one needs to practice and become adept at themselves.

Another story—this one is from Latin America. Eduardo Galeano collects stories and short pieces of wisdom and knowledge scattered across the continents of North, Central, and South America. This one he calls "A Lesson in Medicine" but it could just as easily be called "A Lesson in Listening." This is a story that a man named Ruben Omar Sosa heard about a woman, named Dona Maximiliana, who was a patient in a clinic in Buenos Aires. The course was about doing medicine in the intensive care unit. The student doctors were given the woman's case history in great detail. She was worn out, exhausted, and aging, and had been in the hospital for several days already. He listed her vitals and every day when the doctor came, she would ask the same thing over and over again: "Please, Doctor, could you take my pulse?" And the doctor, medic, or nurse would oblige, taking her thin frail wrist for a moment, fingers on the pulse, with a bit of pressure. And the answer would be given, always in a good range—seventy-five, seventy-eight, eighty—very good really.

Immediately Dona Maximiliana would respond

with her "Thank you, thank you. Now—would you take it again?" The pulse would be taken again and it would, of course, not be that different and he'd respond, "You're fine." This happened day after day, the same scene over and over again, no matter who would come in to check on her. He'd come over to the bed and she'd stick out her stick of an arm and in her wheezing low weak voice ask again, "Please, Doctor, could you take my pulse?" He began to dread going into the room and spending any more time with her than was absolutely necessary, wanting instead to get on about his rounds. He was always polite but he was also thinking, "The old bird is a pain in the neck. She's probably a hypochondriac and is losing it." He told the group after a few moments of awkward silence—it took me years to realize that all she wanted was someone to touch her.[6]

The doctor was so intent on curing, on fixing, on doing his job in medicine that he was reacting to her as an "it," a patient, rather than a person who didn't need his expertise but did need his attention and care. Often-times people come to those with power not for anything in particular but to be treated with respect, dignity, to be listened to and understood and accepted as a person worthy of their time and presence. The focus of many people in power is correcting people whom they perceive as not understanding the teachings or not knowing what they should do. They judge these people in regard to what they have done or didn't do, their situation in life, and whether they adhere to the right dogma and way of doing things. Their power base, be that of work, teaching, or the institution they lead, control, or speak for—whether educational, religious, church, parish, diocese, military—is in the forefront of any relationship; but it is most important that they listen to the person with care, compassion, respect, and integrity than enforce or demand acceptance from their perspective and interest.

For Christians and Catholics, as well as many other religious groups, Jesus has something to say about the attitude of those in authority who claim to be listening, responding, and teaching with the Spirit of God. It bears listening to and applying to all experiences when those with authority and power are supposed to be listening to those who come to them.

> Jesus summoned them and said to them, "You know that those who are recognized as rulers over the Gentiles lord it over them, and their great ones make their authority over them felt. But it shall not be so among you. Rather, whoever wishes to be great among you will be your servant; whoever wishes to be first among you will be the slave of all. For the Son of Man did not come to be served but to serve and to give his life as a ransom for many. (Mark 10:42–45)

Theologically this passage is the basis for all authority and practice of power within the churches, but in reality power rarely is practiced in this vein or style. The concept and practice of being a servant, let alone the slave of all, is alien to those in power, and the structures of the use of power are mostly based in dominance, control, fear, threats, and the use of force to make someone obey rather than with compassion or gentleness of spirit. This is the call to use power the correct way, whether you are the pope, a bishop, the leader of a synagogue, church, mosque, a leader of any religious organization or group or other place of worship; whether you are a pastor or priest, deacon or minister, and whether or not your power is obtained through ordination, educational degree, in-house institution elections, paid professional job and ministry, or personal practice of vocation. Those in religious practice, especially those of Christian traditions, are responsible for those they are in authority over. In fact, up until very recently—the beginning of the twentieth to the twenty-first century—anyone who came for spiritual direction or advice to another shared responsibility for their lives and souls with that person in power when they listened and learned as a devotee, apprentice, or follower, and obeyed what the one in authority above them counseled them to do or practice. It was believed and taught to those in that vocation that while someone was in their counsel, or under their direction and sharing their soul with them, that the one in authority was responsible for any evil or sin that person did—though they were not responsible for any good they did under their influence. This understanding still pervades and is operative in many religious institutions and other groups where the one with power over those under them must account for what is done under their command or influence. (Many religious organizations, churches, and denominations are structured with the presiding bishop, minister, head of religious community, and so on as the corporation sole in legal matters with the ability to hire and fire, shift and reappoint positions, and so on.) The person with more power must keep in mind that their power and control is not just for what goes on between them personally but also when they leave their office, confessional, or place of shared listening.

Again, the difficulty often arises that holding those in power accountable is hard to do; calling them to responsibility, restitution, or restorative justice for their part in what they counsel, teach, and tell others to do in obedience to them is often nearly impossible because of the closed systems this kind of power and authority operate in today's society.

On a positive note, the position of a person with authority over others is a place of privilege and grace that abounds with intimacy and freedom to share in deep places of human life and peoples' deepest hopes. Again, a story can remind us of this reality of being blessed with power over and with others. It is often called "Why Are We Here."

Once upon a time a rabbi was sitting with his students while studying a portion of the Torah. The rabbi reminded them that they were seeking to listen to the Torah and that they were having a conversation with the Scripture as surely as they were having a conversation with another person or even the Holy One. From out of nowhere, one of the students asked the old, clichéd question, "If a tree falls in a forest, does it make a sound?" Everyone was wondering where that came from but they were very intrigued by their master's response. He asked them—back to basics—what is sound? And then he answered his own question. Sound is being able to listen. Sound is a translation between human beings. He said, "So in reply to your question, let me say this— without an ear to register the vibrations of the tree falling and hitting the ground, no sound is produced. Sound is not just a thing. In fact it's not even a thing: it is a translation between human beings—an ear to hear!"

There was silence as the disciples sought to absorb what the master was telling them. But the master continued. "All of the Torah is asking the same question over and over—why are we here? We, human beings are the other half—half of every sound. We are here to hear!" (This is Reb Yerachmiel's teaching.)

Again there was silence until another student said, "But, Rabbi, not only human beings can hear. Dogs can hear things humans can't hear. Birds can hear things we can't hear. All kinds of animals, even fish can hear things we can't hear. What about them—and the fact that we can't hear what they can hear?" The rabbi acknowledged that what the student said was true enough. But he continued. "We, human beings, can hear what even dogs, or birds or trees or anything else that hears can't hear. Listen—we can hear a heart breaking. We can hear the cry for justice and the protest against injustice. We can hear hope stirring. We can hear the call of the Holy One, Blessed Be the Name. We can hear the whisper of empathy and the shiver and silence of death. Think of all the things we can hear that no others can hear. Listen! You are to listen not only to what everyone else can hear but you are also to listen to that which only you can hear. ONLY YOU can hear. Why are we here? We are here to hear and to listen and translate it all to all human beings."

The story is a teaching in itself, layered and dense, but it alerts us once again to how honored and privileged we are to be able to hear others' depths and souls, heart longings and stories. Positions of power often are a doorway, an ear to hear what is not shared otherwise. Our positions in our churches and religion, in our jobs, vocations, and everyday life—because of our knowledge and learning, our life experiences—are an invitation for many to share with us, hoping that we hear, listen, understand, and attend to their lives and hearts. It is our responsibility to attend to them, to witness to their presence and lives and to listen—obey their deepest places of integrity and dignity, need and power.

Perhaps to end this examination of the dynamics of unequal power, we can remember that at our roots we are all equal, all one, all called to be in communion as human beings. In theologies of contemplation, we often only are referring to seeing and listening to God, but what if we learn that contemplation with God most often comes through learning to listen to others? Listen to these words from Thomas Merton as he speaks about contemplation and reflect upon them in terms of how we are called to listen to all other human beings.

Contemplation is also the response to a call: a call from Him Who has no voice, and yet Who speaks in everything that is, and Who, most of all, speaks in the depths of our own being; for we ourselves are words of His. But we are words that are meant to respond to Him, to answer to Him, to echo Him, and even in some way to contain Him. Contemplation is this echo.

We ourselves become His echo and His answer. It is as if in creating us God asked a question and in awakening us to contemplation He answered the question so that the contemplative is at the same time, question and answer.[7]

We are called to listen to others as we listen to who or what we call God, to the earth, our bodies, and our own souls. As we mature as human beings, we must make sure that our capacity to hear, to listen, to attend to others, and to understand others grows apace with our lives, our work, and our power as individuals and as persons with others. Mohsin Hamid, an Islamic scholar, is saying the same thing as Merton: "Empathy is about hearing and finding echoes of another person in yourself."[8] Albert Schweitzer said it this way: "Sometimes our light goes out, but is blown again into instant flame by an encounter with another human being. Each of us owes the deepest thanks to those who have rekindled this inner light."[9] In every moment of listening, we can spark another by our presence and our listening to them.

This chapter is perhaps harder to read and to listen to, and even more so to obey, than some of the others in this book. It was certainly harder to write, and much of what is written has come from other people asking questions and struggling in their own lives to live and listen with more integrity and depth. This story is a good way to end the book and a reminder that true listening is light and free and always based on hope.

In Guatemala, in small villages high up in the mountains, anonymous people spend their days making tiny dolls—about four to seven of them to an equally small box. The dolls are usually no more than an inch high. The box is brightly painted with simple symbols and is either oval or rectangular, with a lid that fits atop the box. The dolls are delicately made from sticks and bits of rags, discarded clothes and materials, and they are as singular as the person who lovingly makes them. Such a box of dolls is often given as a gift when one arrives as a guest or when one leaves to continue on their way. They are called worry dolls. You are to put them by your bedside, and before you go to bed, you open the box and take out the dolls. Then one by one take up a doll and tell it one of your troubles or worries, or something you need to carry and deal with; then, after the doll has heard your words, carefully put it in the box. Do this with each of the dolls, as many dolls as you have worries and concerns, hopes, fears, and dreams. Then put the lid on the box. They don't speak but they do listen, and they hold your words while you sleep until you wake. They heal and help and inspire just by their presence and hearing, by listening and absorbing your words. Once the dolls are safely bedded down for the night, it is time for you to sleep as well. They will greet you in the morning with the dreams and rest of night and the brightness of a new dawn to live more gracefully with others in the world. It's always remembered, though, that there are only so many dolls in the box—rarely more than four or five, at the max seven—when it is given to you. If you have more troubles and worries than that number—then God help you!

Always God is listening to us, to all of us, all ways. Amen.

All of us, made in God's image, are born to listen to one another, to all others, all ways. Amen. Amen. Amen.

NOTES AND SUGGESTIONS FOR PRACTICE

With One or Two Other Persons, or in Small Groups

There are 1,440 minutes in a day. We use about four to five hundred of them at least to sleep...what about the others? Take a few here and there to consciously be aware, to just stop, listen, and be open to absorb, connect, and become more completely present. Do this, especially before beginning a conversation with someone or a new task; or just periodically (once an hour) stop for two to three minutes, breathe and settle yourself, stretch your neck muscles, move your head and just remember you're in your body—not only your mind.

1. When someone is speaking, LISTEN to understand, to comprehend, to get a sense of what is being said and shared. The word *understand* is standing under, as though you are physically carrying someone on

your shoulders—perceiving reality, situations, and others from under them, from their perspective.

2. Let them finish their sentences, their thoughts before reacting or responding. (This is hard!) Studies show that the average amount of time a teacher waits between asking a question and then calling on someone to respond is usually only one second, maybe two! We usually respond to those who react quickly. Next time—in a conversation or when speaking to a group—try to wait seven to ten seconds before indicating that someone should respond. Or if in a group, ask them to take a moment to think about their response, feelings, thoughts, or reactions.

3. When responding, use the pronoun *I*, singular, to own your thoughts, feelings, insights; if with others, try to use their name if you work or are professionally connected to them.

4. If you are not getting what another says, not understanding or losing the train of their words and thoughts, indicate this and ask for clarification, or ask a question to make sure you're on the same track.

5. Learn to live with and appreciate silences, pauses, even a rest in the conversation (pauses in music, between the notes, make the music!) Silences can be awkward—just taking a breath, nervousness, a bit of fear, a sense of lostness, relief, the gelling of an extended idea or feeling. Silences can be "read" and felt.

6. Don't interrupt unless absolutely necessary—if it seems too much all at once, or if you feel like you need to try to repeat what the other is saying so you have a sense that you know what is being shared, use phrases like, "Please repeat that," or "Could you say that another way?" or "Clarify that point, please."

7. LIGHTEN UP! Laugh, learn the art of light-hearted response, when to just breathe, or have everyone get up, stand, and shake it out—move their hands and arms, breathe deeply, exhale (at least three times), stretch, close their eyes, relax, then sit down and begin again.

8. Try not to judge: your face and body language can appear to be listening, even agreeing, but in your head you're thinking of what to say as rebuttal, whether you agree or disagree—try to turn off the voices and words inside your head. Try not to decide if what is being said is good, bad, awful, great, in need of correction, wrong, and so on.

9. Try to treat the other(s) as equal(s), especially in regard to rank, position, religion, education, and privilege, and speak and listen simply as person to person. Akin to this (especially if this is a one-on-one conversation), remember to speak with integrity, honesty, confidentiality, and only share what needs to be shared. Remember, just because something is true, does not mean that it has to be shared, exposed, or spoken.

10. Know when to stop! Enough already. Don't continue to "beat dead horses." Think about a limit on discussion, the conversation, and time. If you are having others discuss among themselves, start to end the segment with words like this: "Take a moment or two to wrap up your conversation," or ask, "Do you need another couple of minutes?" Then suggest each person gather their thoughts for themselves and then begin to ask for responses for discussion in a larger perspective.

11. Don't feel like you have to settle things, try to organize or collect on behalf of the group (if you're leading a discussion), or try to include "new," surprising, engaging, disconcerting, never-thought-of angles that surface. Honor the diversity that emerges, compliment, respond positively if you can. If you're stunned, taken off balance, say so on occasion. Think of the conversation in terms of circles, ovals, and spirals, but come to a focus as needed. If you are one-on-one try to draw things together for closure or a sense of "this is a good place to end for now."

12. Before discussion in a group, state whether or not you're expecting everyone to contribute or if no one will be required to speak. Or ask if everyone could say one word or phrase (perhaps an adjective, adverb, noun, verb, and so on) if you are looking for a wider expression from the group. It also helps if there is a short period of time for each person to talk with the person beside them, or with two others—once they have put into words out loud what they

think, feel, and are wondering, it is easier to share with a larger group.

13. Lastly, try to be aware of your own body language, tone of voice, movement, eye contact, and how you physically react to each person (in a group) or to the person you are listening and speaking with—these expressions reveal assumptions you are making and feelings that you might or might not be aware of within yourself.

SOME PRACTICES TO ENHANCE LISTENING

1. Take at least ten to fifteen minutes in the morning or evening to just stop, sit up straight or in a recliner (or comfortable chair), stand outside or at a window, and just listen to sounds around you and to the silences and absorb them. Don't think about them, just feel and sense them and remember to breathe!

2. Every time you sense yourself looking at your watch or a clock, try to stop for a moment and just listen and breathe...notice how you are feeling in your body and what's in the air around you...only a minute and then go back to what you were engaged in.

3. Before putting the key in the ignition or pushing the button to start your car, or before getting out, stop again, refocus, and listen and then go onto the next thing, relationship, or situation.

4. Pick a time in the day to just turn off your head, drift, feel, and listen. Many classical radio stations do this around 1 p.m. and play a piece of music straight through, no interruptions. Or eat some nuts, a piece of dark chocolate (very good for you), or have tea, coffee, or water and don't do anything else but chew, swallow, taste, and listen.

5. At least once a day go somewhere in the building you work in, or go outside and listen to the weather, to birds, noises, construction, voices, whatever is there—especially the silences—and practice learning the different kinds of silence and noise. Breathe and return.

6. Try to stop for a few minutes (put a note where you'll see it) and listen to your own heart beat and heart rate, to your breathing, and to what's going on in your body—aches, tensions, pressures, and where you're storing things. If sitting, shake your hands and arms—stretch your neck, extend your fingers, bend them, do the same with your feet, calves, legs, and arms (like they say you should do on a plane, or when you're checking your heart rate during exercise). Listen to your body.

7. And lastly and perhaps most importantly, LISTEN TO YOUR SOUL, your SPIRIT, and your HEART, your inner essence, your sense of energy, power, and integrity. If you believe in a personal God then sit or stand in the presence of the Holy and just be in that presence, known, accepted, freed, living, and being.

And be grateful, give thanks, be in awe, and honor your own person, and that of everyone else and of God. This takes practice—try it for ten to fifteen minutes a day.

A FINAL NOTE

A human being is a part of the whole called by us universe, a part limited in time and space. He [or she] experiences himself, his [or her] thoughts and feelings as something separated from the rest, a kind of optical delusion of his [or her] consciousness. This delusion is a kind of prison for us, restricting us to our personal desires and to affection for a few persons nearest to us. Our task must be to free ourselves from this prison by widening our circle of compassion to embrace all living creatures and the whole of nature in its beauty.

—Albert Einstein, as quoted in
The Experience of Insight,
by Joseph Goldstein (Boston:
Shambhala, 1981), 126

QUESTIONNAIRE ON LISTENING

*"It is the province of knowledge to speak.
And it is the privilege of wisdom to listen."*
—Oliver Wendell Holmes

1. On a scale of one to ten what is your hearing now?

2. Do you prefer to communicate for business through phone or e-mail? Why?

3. Which do you prefer when communicating with friends? Why?

4. When you are on the phone, what other activities do you often engage in doing?

5. a. What is your most relaxing kind of music to listen to? Why?

   b. What is a genre of music that you find annoying or don't listen to? Why?

6. Is there a specific noise that you often become aware of while doing other things?

7. Is there a specific sound that you find grating or irritating?

8. Are you aware of a person with whom or a situation in which you have difficulty listening? When do you become aware of this happening?

9. What volume do you usually have your TV, iPad, or mobile device set at? On the available scale are you in the low, medium, or high range?

10. For you—

    a. What is the sound of childhood?

    b. What is the sound of hope?

    c. What is the sound of doubt?

    d. What is the sound of awe?

    e. What is the sound of surety?

    f. What is the sound of lying or dishonesty?

    g. What is the sound of fear?

11. Are you aware of the sounds of fear and anger? How do you delineate between these two when someone is speaking?

12. What three sounds are you most aware of—seizing your attention always? (Note: For those in the military and many others, the first sound was something in the realm of gunshots, a car backfiring, a

loud explosion, or an equally loud tone of voice either commanding or warning, or raised in fear. Generally speaking it was only women who mentioned a crying child—and usually only those who were mothers).

13. What kind of silence do you find threatening?

14. What kind of silence do you find stilling, deepening, or comforting?

15. Do you associate the loudness of someone's voice with a particular emotion or attitude, such as anger, arrogance, opinionated, demanding? If so, do you know why—what is the root of this association?

16. Do you know what your own voice sounds like—on a tape, a telephone answering machine, on a phone, with and without amplification?

17. Are you aware of having different speaking voices depending upon whom it is that you are speaking with or to—and on how many people are listening? How would you describe these voices?

18. Using adjectives, how would you describe your own voice? (Then ask others—friends, coworkers, family members, even how strangers would describe your voice.)

LITANY FOR LISTENING!

There are Truths beyond self-evident that are core
    and universal,
blood bonds as close and intimate as sinews,
    limbs, and nerves.
We live here. We listen here.
We forget rain, clouds, weather are our siblings.
Stone, river, cactus, all their fellow species are kin.
Four-legged, winged ones, things that crawl, soar,
    dip, dive, swim, breathe—
All are relatives.
This is home. We listen here.
Each parcel, acre, corner, crevice, all unmappable,
    no borders, boundaries—
Just home, where everyone must be taken in,
    welcomed to dwell, listened to with attention.

Tree talkers, wind singers, tracks, sign languages
    and dialects,
even mute and wordless expressions keep trying
    to speak to us.
Look! Listen! they say.
The flowers are offered. The greens are returning.

First nights are appearing—spring, rain, warm
    summer winds...then they change
tactics with the cold coming around a corner, back
    and burrowing in for a long stay.
Try again: leaves and limbs, blossoms, dusk,
    temperatures falling.

We're all made of the same "stuff"—stardust,
    molecules, energy, shifting matter,
rearrangements with a bit of sugar water thrown
    in for longer life.
Even the endless greens: cottonwood, chamisa,
    sage, pine, palm, mesquite, maple, oak,
    evergreen, scrub, sycamore, cypress, conifer.
Every shade and hue of sky or ground, even air
    that is visible, pulsing, reflecting
    and odiferous! Oddities of creation and
        humankind all with their presences say:
        Listen to me!

I wonder, God, do you ever miss being human,
    limited but in awe of limitless
Revelations of who you are with all your
    thousand and one names and then in the names
    each of us whisper, announce, sing, cry out,
    stand wordless with our presences here, waiting
    to be heard, listened to, cherished and repeated
    in others' voices?

Did you ever long to stay?
Or do you secretly return on some dark nights
    when even the moon hides her face?
I would like to think that incarnation sleeps deep
    in your bones and tingles in your spirit
—even now—whatever you are and wherever you
    dwell, everywhere you linger, hide, and wait to
    be found.
You know, Holy One, I have ever longed to stand
    hand in hand with you.
Reveling in your world, leaving it all unspoken,
    just holding hands with you and all your
    people, your children, your friends,
as one, listening here...just being, listening. Amen

NOTES

INTRODUCTION

1. Maya Angelou, *I Know Why the Caged Bird Sings* (New York: Random House, 2002), 95.

2. Terry Tempest Williams, *When Women Were Birds: Fifty-four Variations on Voice* (New York: Picador, 2013), chap. 49.

3. Walking Buffalo in Grant MacEwan, *Tatanga Mani: Walking Buffalo of the Stonies* (Edmonton, Canada: M. G. Hurtig, 1969), 5, 181.

4. Wendell Berry, "To Know The Dark," in *Farming: A Hand Book* (Berkeley: Counterpoint, 2011), 26.

5. Obtained from notes on the CD cover.

1. LISTENING – HEARING

1. American Association of Retired Persons, 2013.

2. Bella Bathurst, "Sound Advice," *Aeonmagazine*, published online (February 8, 2013), http://www.aeon magazine.com/oceanic-feeling/bella-bathurst-listening-silence/.

3. Susan Stewart, quoted in *On Being with Krista Tippet*, February 1, 2014.

2. BEGINNING

1. See, for example, Teresa A. Keenan, "The State of Hearing Health: A Study of AARP Members," *AARP.org*, December 2011, http://www.aarp.org/health/conditions-treatments/info-12-2011/hearing-issues.html.

2. University of Missouri Extension, CM150, *Listening: Our Most Used Communication Skill* (October 1993): first paragraph, http://extension.missouri.edu/publications.

3. Found in a shortened form in the *Pirkei Avot: The Ethics of the Fathers* 5:18.

4. Eckhart Tolle, art by Patrick McDonnell, *Guardians of Being: Spiritual Teachings from Dogs and Cats* (Novato, CA: New World Library, 2009), 26.

5. Henning Mankell, translated from the Swedish by Tiina Nunnally.

3. LISTENING TO THE TEXTS

1. F. Max Muller, *Introduction to the Science of Religion* (London: Longmans Green and Co., 1873), 16.

2. Yanki Tauber, "Second Chapter of the Shema," *Chabad.org* (date unknown), http://www.chabad.org/parshah/article_cdo/aid/53667/jewish/The-Second-Chapter.htm.

3. Hasidic Tale, told by Jacob Needleman.

4. Marjorie J. Thompson, "Obedience: The Deepest Passion of Love," *Weavings* 26, no. 2 (May/June 1988): 36.

5. Chris Chivers, *Thirst for Life: CAFOD/Christian*

Aid Lent Book (London: Darton, Longman and Todd, 2007).

4. FROM HEART-TO-HEART TO SOUL-TO-SOUL

1. *Kitchen Table Wisdom: Stories That Heal* (New York: Riverhead, 2006).

2. Alireza Nurbakhsh, "Friendship," *Sufi Journal* 82 (Winter 2012): 8.

3. Adapted from Lo Wing Huen and Sun Li Jie, "Looking in One's Mirror," in *Best Chinese Idioms*, 3 (Hong Kong: Hai Feng Publishing, 1997).

4. Rachel Naomi Remen, *Kitchen Table Wisdom* (New York: Riverhead Books, 1996), 219.

5. See "Listening Generously: The Medicine of Rachel Naomi Remen," *On Being with Krista Tippett*, Speaking of Faith, November 27, 2008, http://www.onbeing.org/program/listening-generously/transcript/4418.

6. Ibid.

7. Tzvi Freeman, *Bringing Heaven Down to Earth: Meditations and Everyday Wisdom from the Teachings of the Rebbe Menachem Schneerson* (Avon, MA: Adams Media Corp., 1999).

5. SILENCE

1. Henry David Thoreau, *The Writings of Henry David Thoreau, Journal I: 1837-1846*; quote in entry of December 18, 1838 (Boston: Houghton Mifflin, 1906), 64.

2. Christopher Jamison, "Vital Changes Can Be

Framed by Silence as well as by Fanfares," *The Tablet*, January 1, 2011, 5.

3. W. B. Yeats, *The Celtic Twilight* (London: A. H. Bullen, 1912), 128.

4. Yanki Tauber, *Beyond the Letter of the Law: A Chassidic Companion to the Talmud's Ethics of the Fathers* (Brooklyn, NY: Meaningful Life Center, 2012).

5. Thomas Kelly, in *A Testament of Devotion*, quoted by Peter Lang, in *Friends Journal* 56, no. 11 (December 2010): 22.

6. Etty Hillesum, *An Interrupted Life and Letters from Westerbork* (New York: Henry Holt & Co., 1996), August 26, 1941 journal entry.

7. From "The 'Sound' Path to Meditation," The Institute for Contemplative Practice, the Weekly Reflection for September 24, 2013.

8. Thierry Gosset, ed., "Edith Stein," in *Women Mystics of the Contemporary Era: 19th–20th Centuries* (Strathfield, Australia: St. Paul Publications, 2003), 156.

9. Ibid.

10. As published in "Main," *Hasidic Tales*, July 12, 2010, https://hasidictales.wordpress.com/2010/07/17/.

11. Enzo Bianchi, *Words of Spirituality: Exploring the Inner Life*, 2nd ed., trans. Christine Landau (London: SPCK, 2012), 72.

12. Dietrich Bonhoeffer, quoted in Enzo Bianchi, *Echoes of the Word: A New Kind of Monk on the Meaning of Life* (Brewster, MA: Paraclete, 2013), 112–13.

13. Ibid., 111.

14. Father Paschal, custodian of the Merton Hermitage, Gethsemani, Kentucky, in a conversation

with John Dear in *The Sound of Listening: A Retreat Journal from Thomas Merton's Hermitage* (New York: Continuum, 1999), 55–56.

6. MUSIC AND NOISE

1. Maureen Nandini Mitra, "Extremely Loud," *Earth Island Journal* 28, no. 1 (March 5, 2013), http://www.earthisland.org/journal/index.php/eij/article/extremely_loud/.
2. Ibid.
3. Ibid.
4. Maya Angelou, *Even the Stars Look Lonesome* (New York: Random House, 1997), 36–37.

7. LISTENING WITH HOPE

1. Ellis Peters, *The Sanctuary Sparrow: The Seventh Chronicle of Brother Cadfael, of the Benedictine Abbey of Saint Peter and Saint Paul, at Shrewsbury* (London: Macmillan, 1983), 1.
2. Academy of Achievement, interview with Elie Wiesel, June 29, 1996, Sun Valley, ID, http://www.achievement.org/autodoc/printmember/wie0int-1.
3. Elie Wiesel, Nobel Peace Prize Acceptance Speech, December 10, 1986, quoted from a sign found in a synagogue.
4. Rabbi Joachim Prinz, President of the American Jewish Congress, speech at March on Washington, August 28, 1963, http://www.joachimprinz.com/civilrights.htm.

5. Elsa Tamez, "From the Archives: September 1986," *Sojourners* (September/October 2010), https://sojo.net/magazine/septemberoctober-2010/archives-september-1983.

6. Arthur Schopenhauer, *Parerga and Paralipomena: Short Philosophical Essays*, trans. E. F. J. Payne, vol. 2 (New York: Oxford University Press, 1974), 651.

7. Eduardo Galeano, "Walls," in *Mirrors: Stories of Almost Everyone*, trans. Mark Fried (New York: Nation Books, 2009), 336.

8. *The Constitution of the Iroquois Nations: The Great Binding Law, Gayanashagowa*, no. 28, see http://www.constitution.org/cons/iroquois.htm.

9. Richard M. Kelly, "Truth as a Moving Target on a Local Train," *Friends Journal* (December 2011): 16.

8. LET THERE BE NIGHT!

1. Translation is from The Jewish Study Bible: Tanakh Translation, The Jewish Publication Society (New York: Oxford University Press, 2004), 12.

2. The BOSS survey was completed following the writing of this book. See "Baryon Oscillation Spectroscopic Survey Measures the Universe to One-Percent Accuracy," *Phys.org*, January 8, 2014, http://phys.org/news/2014-01-baryon-oscillation-spectroscopic-survey-universe.html.

3. Note: on days two and four, those words are omitted, but then those words appear twice on day three and on the day that we are brought forth.

4. Nicholas King, trans., *The New Testament* (Suffolk, England: Kevin Mayhew, Ltd., 2005).

9. LISTENING TO YOUR BODY

1. August Rodin and Paul Gsell, *Art: Conversations with Paul Gsell*, trans. Jacques de Caso and Patricia B. Sanders (Los Angeles: University of California Press, 1984), 51–52.

2. Thomas Merton, *The Collected Poems of Thomas Merton* (New York: New Directions, 1977), 363.

3. Walt Whitman, *The Complete Poems of Walt Whitman* (Hertfordshire, England: Wordsworth Editions, 1995), 88.

4. Abraham Heschel, *Between God and Man: An Interpretation of Judaism* (New York: Free Press, 1997), 37.

5. Martin Luther King Jr., as quoted in Charles R. Johnson, "The King We Need," *Lion's Roar*, January 16, 2016, http://www.lionsroar.com/the-king-we-need-charles-r-johnson-on-the-legacy-of-dr-martin-luther-king-jr/#.

6. This quote was taken from David Steindl-Rast's website *Gratefulness.org*.

10. LISTENING TO THE EARTH—TO THE UNIVERSE

1. William Wordsworth, "Composed a Few Miles above Tintern Abbey, on Revisiting the Banks of the Wye during a Tour, July 13, 1978," in *Lyrical Ballads* (London: J. & A. Arch, 1978), lines 101–3, http://www.

rc.umd.edu/sites/default/RCOldSite/www/rchs/reader/t abbey.html.

2. Pierre Teilhard de Chardin, "Sketch of a Personalistic Universe" (1936), in *Human Energy*, vol. 6 of the completed works (Paris: Editions du Seuil, 1955), 23.

3. Recipient of the 1945 Nobel Prize for Physics for the Pauli exclusion principle, in Norman Friedman, *Bridging Science and Spirit* (St. Louis: Living Lake Books, 1990).

4. In Pierre Teilhard de Chardin, *The Phenomenon of Man* (New York: Harper Perennial, 2008), 26.

5. For reference and an extended introduction and overview of the man and his work, see Dave Pruett, *Reason and Wonder: A Copernican Revolution in Science and Spirit* (Santa Barbara, CA: ABC-CLIO/Praeger, 2012), also the papers from the Spirit of Fire Conference, held at Chestnut Hill College, Philadelphia, PA, 2005.

6. Walt Whitman, "Son of the Open Road," in *Leaves of Grass: The First (1855) Edition* (New York: Classic Book Int., 2010), 93.

7. Ernesto Cardenal, Abide in Love (New York: Orbis Books, 1995) quoted in *The Tablet*, April 14, 2012, 17.

8. These quotes by Thomas Merton were taken from the daily reflections by the Thomas Merton Institute at *mertoninstitute.org*. Unfortunately, the institute ceased operations at the end of 2012.

11. LISTENING IN RELATIONSHIPS
OF UNEQUAL POWER

1. Alan Alda, *Never Have Your Dog Stuffed: And Other Things I've Learned* (New York: Random House, 2005).

2. As quoted in "The Promise of Listening" in *The Wisdom of Listening*, ed. Mark Brady (Boston, MA: Wisdom Publications, 2003), 4.

3. *I and Thou* (New York: Charles Scribner's Sons, 1951).

4. "The Mathnawi of Jalaluddin Rumi."

5. Stories such as this can be found in collections of Zen stories, such as Richard McLean, *Zen Fables for Today*, (New York: Avon Books, 1998).

6. Eduardo Galeano, *Voices of Time: A Life in Stories*, trans. Mark Fried (New York: Henry Holt and Company, 2006), 226.

7. *New Seeds of Contemplation* (New York: New Directions Books, 1961), 3.

8. Mohsin Hamid, "The New Yorker," September 12, 2012.

9. Albert Schweitzer, *Out of My Life and Thought: An Autobiography.*